PROFESSOR BLOOMER'S
NO-NONSENSE
BASIC READING PROGRAM:

A SIMPLIFIED
PHONETIC APPROACH

STUDENTS LEARNING BOOK
Volume 2
Fifth Edition

RICHARD H. BLOOMER, ED.D.
Emeritus Professor
The University of Connecticut

Copyright 1956, 1968, 1973, 2002, 2017

IBSN 978 09840295-9-4

Beginning Reading, Home-Schooling, Writing, Spelling, independence, First Grade, Kindergarten, Education,

Acknowledgments

This work is hardly mine alone. It rests on the work of many scholars and scientists reaching back into antiquity.

The ancient Phoenicians knew that by mastering Letter/sounds and putting them together to make spoken words, readers could obtain meaning from written words. Once the visual word is encoded into speech, meaning or understanding is a separate and very different set of mental processes contingent upon the learner's prior experiences.

At Teachers College, Edward L. Thorndike and Irving Lorge shaped my scientific attitude. Robert S. Woodworth never let me forget that there is an "Orgamism" between the "Stimulus" and the "Response." Percival Symonds provided encouraging mentorship and laboratory space for my early experiments in human learning.

I wish to thank the folks at Central Institute for the Deaf, for simplifying the standard phonetic alphabet to make it much simpler and more useful for students to learn their letter/sounds

All research tracks need an initial stimulus. Mine was provided by my friend Myron Woolman, whose early case studies in teaching adult reading prompted me to research and refine those seminal ideas into a systematic, integrated language teaching program for children.

Most important, an exceptional teacher, Frances Little, who adopted the first edition of this integrated language program, had the courage to go against the educational trends and her peers, and whose pupils never failed to succeeded in reading during her twenty-seven years as a first-grade teacher.

To Dr. Ann Marie Bernaza-Haase, who was instrumental in shaping my musings into the Reading/Typing Program and developed many of the stories and workbook materials that made these readers possible

To my supportive partner, Jan Maya Schold, who gives me the space to think and create and an occasional jog to spur me on and chipped in many of her precious hours to find and correct my many mistakes

Many of the illustrations were done by our wonderful local artist and calligrapher, Kathy LePack

Much Credit must be given to Dover publications and the Nova Development company of California for generous permission to use their royalty free images.

Within my personal experience. my grandfather Hermon Hutcheson drilled into my preadolescent mind his mantra "There ain't no such word as can't."

Last, and perhaps most important, was my own wicked step mother, Marguerite Barnes Bloomer, who with boundless patience first taught me "how" to learn. She also taught me, that "Learning is not fun." Learning is hard work; it is the accomplishment that is rewarding.

"Once you learn to read, you will be forever free."

— Frederick Douglass

CONTENTS

Professor Bloomers No-Nonsense Reading Program
Students WorkBook

Preface to the fifth edition

"Literacy is the most important factor in building and preserving our civilization, and teaching children to read is the most important task of our schools. We perform this task clumsily and with great waste of labor and time. Even at the end of eight years many of our pupils cannot be said to read; yet eight months ought to suffice." (Bloomfield, 1942)

I first wrote this program in 1952 as a guide for my students for a remedial reading clinic as a part of a reading methods class. We had sufficient success with that approach that school principals asked us to return year after year. One teacher used the guide for her first grade class and had excellent results The present program was written adapted for the classroom from that original guide in the academic year 1956-57.

The teacher who first used Professor Bloomer's No-Nonsence Reading Program as a first grade classroom reading method back in 1957, every single child she taught, achieved above second grade level, for her whole twenry-seven year teaching career. Another school using this program, in addition to averaging one full grade level above pupils taught using a standard commercal curriculum, reduced referrals for Special Education by 65% and the positive effects of Professor Bloomer's No-Nonsense Reading Program lasted at least until grade seven.

In the clinic at The University of Connecticut we have used Professor Bloomer's Reading Program successfully with dyslexics, children with learning diabilities, speech difficulties, brain damage, and ADHD. During the intervening years we have found that Professor Bloomers No-Nonsense Reading Program works as well with non-English speakers in Latin America and China as long as their instructor speaks English.

Over the last sixty years the quality of public school children's reading has diminished steadily. The many "Reading Plans," periodically put forward are acts of desperation, and have little effect on this downward slide in children's reading skills. It is this same desperation felt by the parents who bring their children to me for help that has prompted this fourth edition of Professor Bloomer's No-Nonsense Reading Program for Young Learners.

Professor Bloomer's No-Nonsense Reading Program is designed using the neuro-science of learning as a step by step plan for parents and teachers to help children through the stages of early reading. The program is focused specifically toward reading independence and the learners abilities to figure out new words on their own. Once these skills are mastered the learner is ready to explore the wide range of learning possibilities offered by additional schooling.

RHB
Wilimantic, CT
2017

A

PICTURES TO LABEL

T

I will be good

PICTURES TO LABEL

A YY I CCCC CC NN

The Wolf

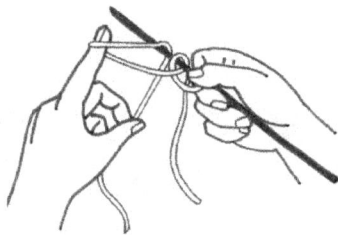

A	AT	TAT	**A**
AT	TAT	**AT**	A
TAT	**TAT**	A	AT

S

_____

_____

2. PICTURES TO LABEL

FIND THE LETTER

S	AT	SAT
T	SAT	AS
S	A	AS
T	A	SAT
T	AT	AS

MATCHING EXERCISE

SAT	TAT
A	AT
AT	AS
TAT	SAT
AS	A

FIND THE WORD AND READ ALOUD

A	TAT	SAT	A
AS	AT	AS	SAT
AT	SAT	AT	TAT
TAT	TAT	AS	SAT
SAT	AT	SAT	TAT

DICTATION

M

PICTURES TO NAME

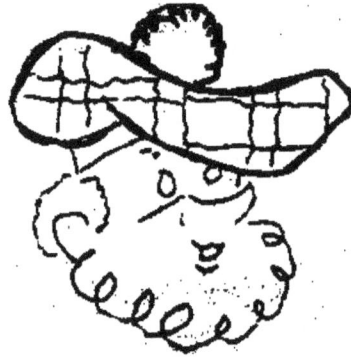

FIND THE LETTER

M	AT	SAM	SAT
S	MAT	TAT	MAST
M	MAMA	AT	MAST
T	SAM	MST	MAMA
M	SAT	AS	MAST

MATCH AND LABEL

SAM
MAMA
MAT
TAM
MAST

MATCHING WORDS

AM	MAST
MAMA	AT
MAT	MAM
MAST	MAMA
TAM	AM
MAM	TAM

FINDING WORD AND READING ALOUD

AM	MAMA	SAM	AM
SAM	SAM	TAM	SAT
MAST	TAM	MAST	TAT
MAMA	MAT	SAT	MAMA
TAM	SAM	TAM	TAT

DICTATION

R

PICTURES TO NAME

MATCH LABEL

TRAM
TAM
RAM
STAR
MAST
RAT
ART
TART

FIND THE LETTER

R	MAT	RAT	SAT
S	TAR	RAM	STAR
T	TAM	SAM	RAT
R	MAMA	TAR	MAM
M	RAM	START	TART
R	SAM	AM	RAM

MATCHING WORDS

RAT	RAM
STAR	START
TAR	RAT
TRAM	TRAM
START	TAM
TAM	TAR
RAM	STAR

FINDING WORDS

RAM	RAT	RAM	MAT
RAT	START	ART	RAT
TAR	TRAM	TAR	RAT
STAR	STAR	START	TART
ART	STAR	TRAM	ART

DICTATION

_____

_____

_____

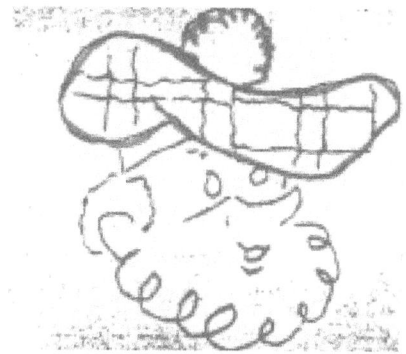

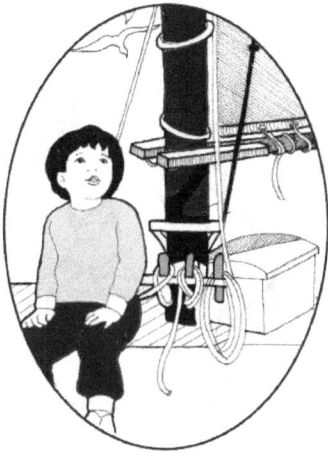

G

PICTURES TO NAME

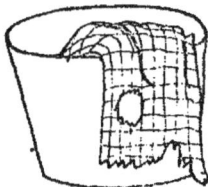

MATCH AND LABEL

GAS
TAG
STAR
TRAM
RAM
GRASS
STAR

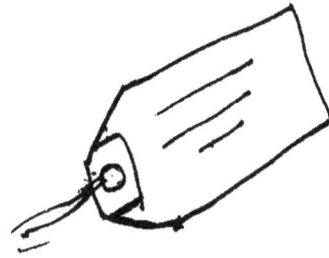

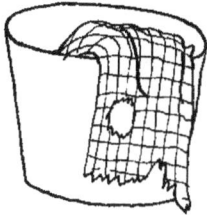

FIND THE LETTER

G	GAS	STAR	RAG
T	TAG	SAG	GAS
M	RAM	MAT	TAG
G	TRAM	GRASS	SAM
R	STAR	MAMA	TART
G	RAG	RAT	GRASS

MATCHING WORDS

TRAM	RAG
RAM	GRASS
GAS	RAM
RAG	GAS
GRASS	TRAM
SAG	TAG
TAG	SAG

FINDING WORD PAIRS

RAG	GRASS	MAT	GRASS
RAG	SAG	RAG	RAG
GAS	GRASS	TRAM	GAS
SAG	TAG	SAG	TAM
TAG	RAM	SAG	TAG
GAG	TAG	RAG	GAG

SOUNDS IN WORDS

RATS	TAM	STAR
RAM	GRASS	TAG
TARTS	GAS	MAST
SAG	TRAM	TART
MAST	MAMA	STAR
TRAM	TAGS	RAT
RAGS	RAM	TAM
MAST	MAST	GAS

DICTATION

HOW MANY WORDS CAN YOU MAKE?
G, T, R, A, S, M,

F

PICTURES TO NAME

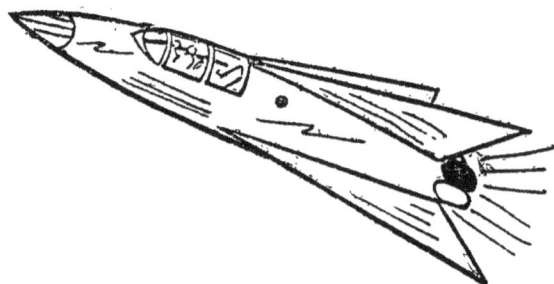

MATCH AND LABEL

FARM
FAST
FAT
TRAM
STAR
RAFT
GAS
TAM
RAT
FAR

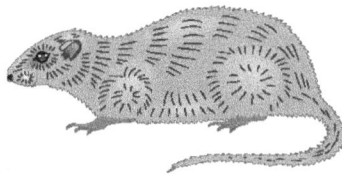

21

FIND THE LETTER

R	SAT	TAM	FARM
T	FAR	STAR	RAM
M	FAT	TRAM	SAM
G	MAMA	SAG	RAFT
T	GAS	MAT	TRAM
F	TART	FAR	RAG
M	RAT	MAT	SAT
F	GRASS	RAFT	MAST

MATCHING WORDS

FAR	FAST
FAST	FAR
RAFT	FARM
FAT	GRASS
FARM	FAT
GRASS	RAFT

FINDING WORD PAIRS

FAST	FAT	FAT	FAR
FAST	FAR	FAST	GRAMA
RAT	RAT	RAG	FAT
RAFT	MAT	MAST	RAFT
RAT	FARM	FAT	FARM
FAR	FARM	MAR	FAR

SOUNDS IN WORDS

RATS	TAM	FARM
RAFT	GRASS	TAGS
TARTS	GAS	MAST
SAG	TRAMS	FAST
MAST	MAMA	FRAM
TRAMS	TAGS	RAFT
RAGS	RAM	TAM
FAST	TAM	SAT

DICTATION

HOW MANY WORDS CAN YOU MAKE?
T, S, A, M, F, G, R

PHRASES TO READ ALOUD AND WRITE

FAT SAM _____

A FAT RAT _____

A FAT RAM _____

SAM'S RAFT _____

A FAST TRAM _____

FAST SAM _____

FAT SAM SAT _____

A FAST RAT _____

A FAST RAFT _____

A FAT RAT SAT _____

COMPLETING PHRASES

A _AST RAT.

SAM'S _AFT.

A _AT RAM.

PICTURES TO LABEL

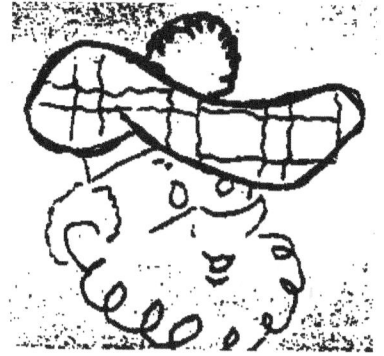

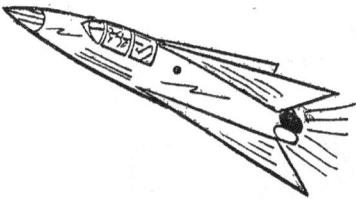

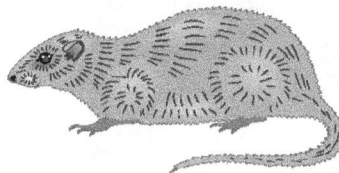

W

PICTURES TO NAME

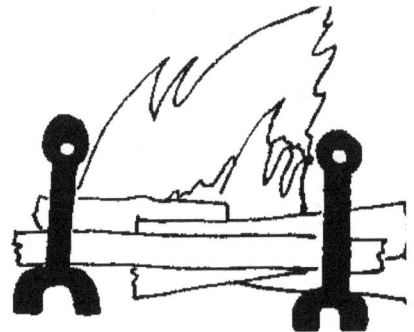

PICTURES TO NAME

FIND THE LETTER

W	SWAM	SAT	TRAM
F	RAFT	SAW	WAR
R	GAS	FAT	GRASS
G	TAR	TAGS	SAW
W	SAG	RAFT	WARM
S	TART	SAW	FARM
W	WARM	STAR	FAST
G	FAT	WAG	GAS

MATCHING WORDS

STRAW	WARM
SAW	WAG
WAG	STRAW
RAW	WAR
WAS	SAW
WARM	RAW
WAR	WAS

FINDING WORDS/READING ALOUD

SAM	MAT	RAM	FAR
RAW	WAR	RAW	WARM
WAS	WAS	SAM	WAS
WARM	WAG	RAG	WAG
WAS	WARM	STRAW	STRAW
WAR	WAS	SAW	WAR
SWAM	WARM	WARM	FARM

FLASH IDENTIFICATION

RAW	MAT	RAM	FAR
SAW	RAM	MAR	RAW
RAM	RAT	SAT	GRASS
WAR	FARM	WARM	SWAM
FAT	SAM	SAW	WARM
WAR	WARM	RAFT	SWAM

SOUNDS IN WORDS

RAG	WARM	SAT
TAGS	SAW	TAR
WAR	GAS	START
STAR	SAW	FAR
TAG	FAST	MAST
WAS	STAR	TAG
ART	GAS	WAG
RAT	WARM	SAW

DICTATION

_____

_____

_____

WHAT IS THIS? CAN YOU MAKE IT BETTER?

CAN YOU DRAW IT EVEN BETTER DOWN HERE?

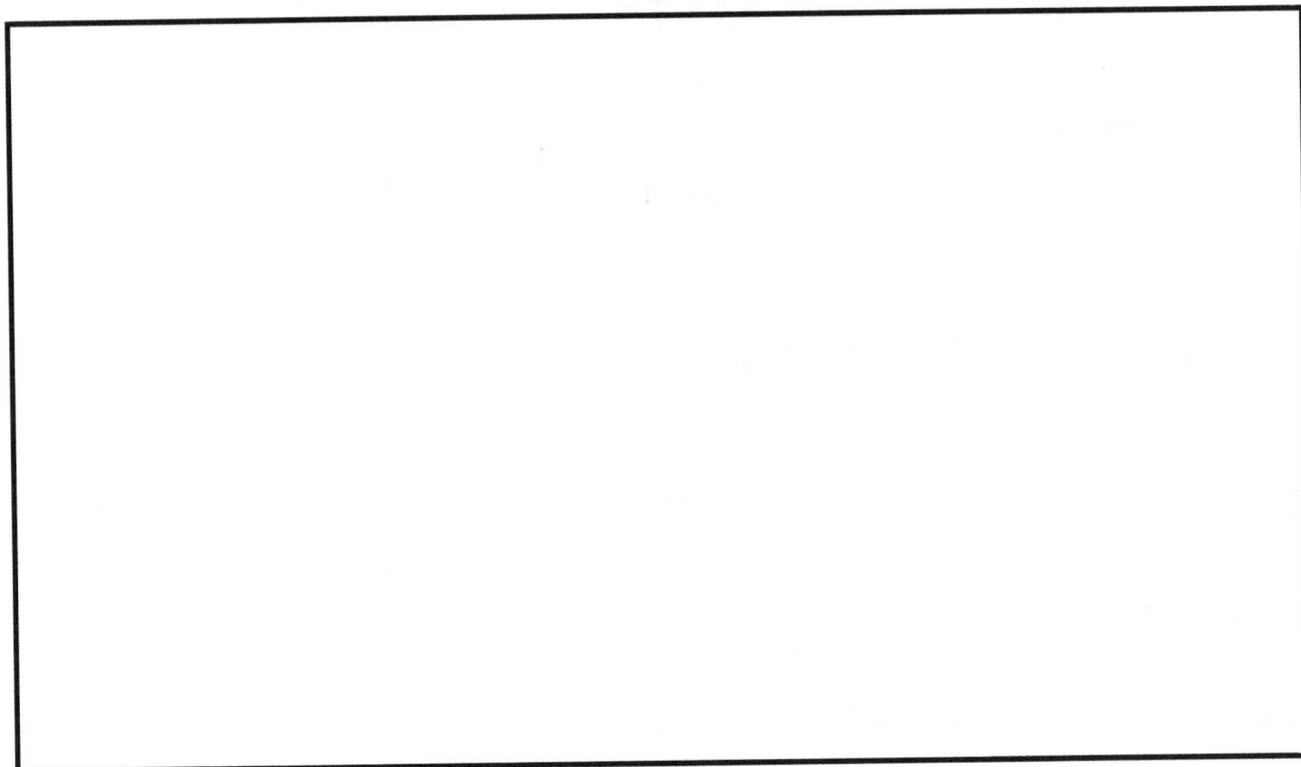

HOW MANY WORDS CAN YOU MAKE
T, R, A, F, W, M, S.

PHRASES TO COPY AND READ ALOUD

A RAT WAS FAST._____

SAM WAS AT A FARM _____

SAM WAS FAT AND FAST._____

SAM SAW A RAM._____

A RAT SAW SAM_____

A RAM SAW GRASS. _____

A RAT SAW A RAFT. _____

MAMA SAW A STAR._____

A RAT SWAM._____

COMPLETING SENTENCES

SAM WAS __ARM
SAM SA__ A RA__T
SAM S__AM AT A __AFT.

PICTURE PHRASES

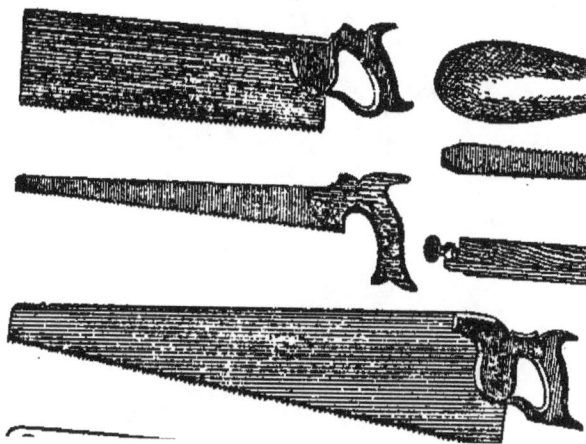

D

_____

_____

PICTURES TO LABEL

MATCH AND LABEL

DART
FAST
FAT
DAM
SAT
DAD
TAG
MAMA
DRAG
MAD

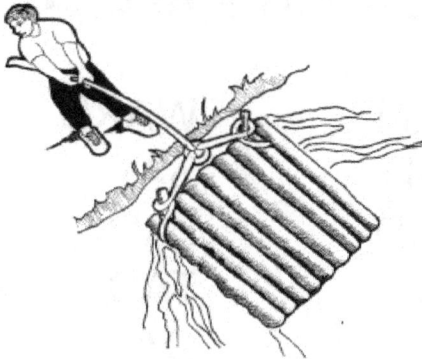

FIND THE LETTER

D	RAFT	FAST	ADD
S	TAGS	RAW	DAM
F	ART	FAR	SAD
W	SAT	MAT	WARM
M	MAD	RAT	TAM
D	WAR	DAD	SAT
S	AS	FAT	SAT
D	SAG	AM	SAD

MATCHING WORDS

DAD	DRAG
DAM	SAD
DART	MAD
TAD	TAD
SAD	DAD
DRAG	DART
MAD	DAM

FINDING WORDS/READING ALOUD

DAD	DAD	DAM	WARD
DRAM	SAT	SAD	SAT
MAD	TAD	MAD	FAD
DAD	TAD	SAD	TAD
DART	WARD	WARD	DAD
MAD	DAM	SAM	MAD
SAD	ADD	FAD	ADD

FLASH IDENTIFICATION

TAD	SAD	MAD	SAT
DRAG	TAMS	DRAFT	DAM
DART	SAT	MAD	DRAG
FAT	DART	SAG	FARM
SAG	SAD	DRAG	TAD
DAM	WAS	RATS	SAM
SAG	MAT	SAW	FAT
DART	TAG	TAD	DRAG

SOUNDS IN WORDS

SAG	ADD	SWAM
DAM	FAST	WAR
SAD	MAD	RAFTS
GRASS	FAD	SAD
SAG	FAR	DAD
SAT	TAT	SAD
DART	GAS	MAST
FAD	FAR	SAD

DICTATION

_____

_____

_____

WHAT IS THIS? CAN YOU MAKE IT BETTER?

CAN YOU DRAW IT EVEN BETTER DOWN HERE?

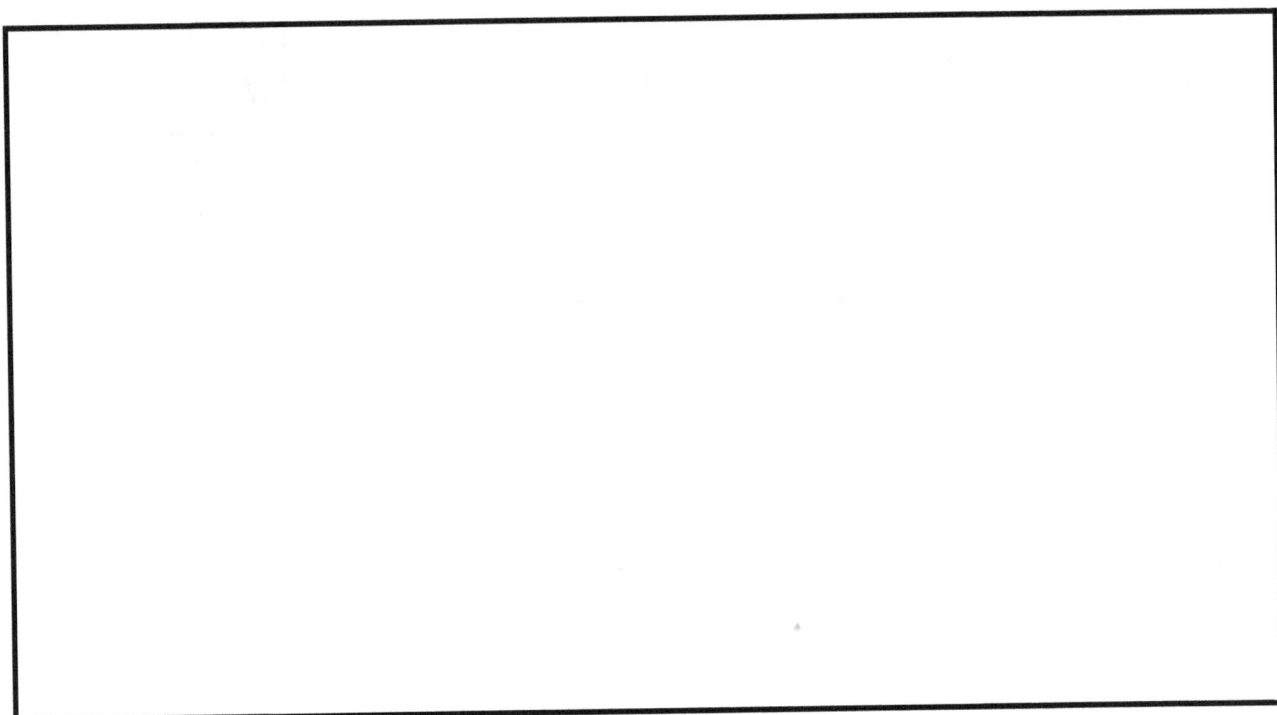

HOW MANY WORDS CAN YOU MAKE
D, W, A, S, M, T, R

PHRASES TO COPY AND READ ALOUD

DAD WAS MAD_____

DAD WAS SAD._____

DAD SAW SAM._____

SAM WAS SAD._____

DAD SAW MAM_____

MAMA WAS WARM._____

MAMA WAS MAD AT DAD _____

_____

COMPLETING SENTENCES

SAM SA-   A DAR_
_AMA WAS -ARM
MAMA   _AW A RAF_
MAMA SWA_ AT A RA_T
A _AT RAT S_AM AT A _AFT

PICTURE PHRASES

PICTURE PHRASES

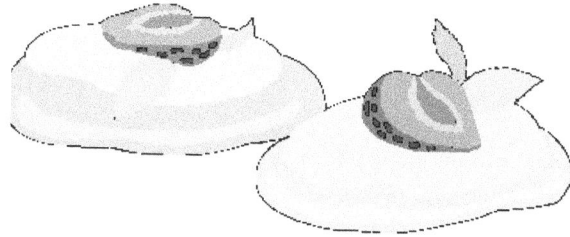

N_____

_____

PICTURES TO LABEL

MATCH AND LABEL

FAN
DAM
ANT
RAM
RAN
MAN
SANTA
GRAMA
NAN

FIND THE LETTER

N	ANTS	AN	TAG
D	DART	SAW	AND
R	SAND	RAN	FAST
D	FANS	RAT	NAT
N	AND	STRAW	DAN
G	ART	GRASS	TAGS
W	TAN	WANT	SAND
N	ANTS	WAR	NAN

MATCHING WORDS

AN	SAND
ANT	DAN
DAN	AND
FAN	SANTA
AND	ANT
WANT	AN
SAND	FAN
RAN	WANT
SANTA	RAN

FINDING THE WORD/READING ALOUD

SAM	WANT	SWAN	WANT
SAND	SAND	NAT	MAT
NAT	WAND	ANT	ANT
AND	SANTA	SWAN	AND
TAN	AND	TAN	DAN
DAN	DAN	NAG	WANT
TAN	SWAN	FAN	FAN
WAND	NAN	WAND	DAN
WANT	RAN	SAM	RAN
SWAN	SWAN	TAN	WAND

FLASH IDENTIFICATION

WAND	SWAN	TAN	SAND
SAND	NAT	ANT	SAM
FAN	AND	AND	DAN
DAN	FAN	SWAN	WAND
AND	WAND	DAN	SANTA
WANT	RAN	WAND	RAT
RAN	SAM	AN	WANT
SAND	WAND	SWAM	AN

SOUNDS IN WORDS

NAN	WANT	DART
SAND	AN	WANT
SAT	WAND	RAN
AND	STAR	ART
WAG	GRASS	ANTS
DAN	FAN	SAND
FACT	RAN	AND
NAN	SAW	FAN

DICTATION

_____

_____

_____

HOW MANY WORDS CAN YOU MAKE
D, S, N, W, A, T, F, R.

WHAT IS THIS? CAN YOU MAKE IT BETTER?

CAN YOU MAKE IT BETTER DOWN HERE?

PHRASES TO COPY AND READ ALOUD

NAN SAW ANTS._____

DAN SAW A SWAN._____

NAN AND NAT RAN._____

DAN AND NAN SAW SANTA._____

_____

DAN SAW A TAN RAT._____

A TAN RAT WANTS A TART._____

_____

MAMA WAS WARM._____

MAMA WANTS A FAN._____

COMPLETING SENTENCES

A RAT RA_
DAN SAW A FA_.
NAT S-W SA-TA
A RA_ AND A_ ANT SWAM
DAD SA_   A MAN AND A SWA_.
A S_AN SWAM FA_T
A _AM RAN AT D_N.

PICTURE PHRASES

U

PICTURES TO LABEL

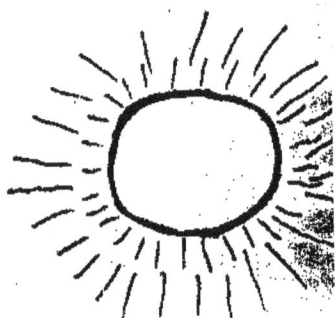

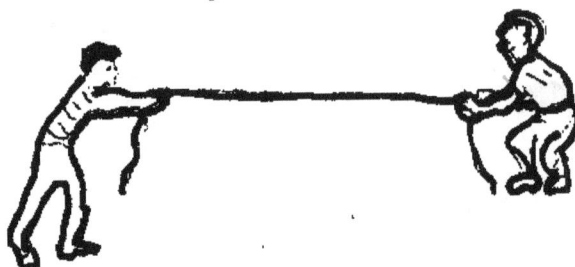

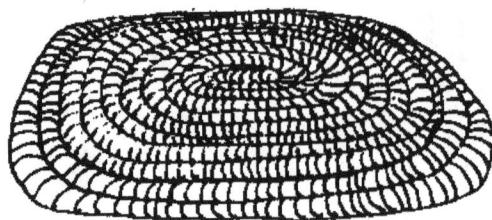

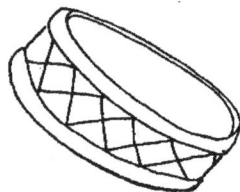

MATCH AND LABEL

DRUM
SUN
FARM
RAT
FUN
DUG
NUT
FAN
TAG
DUST

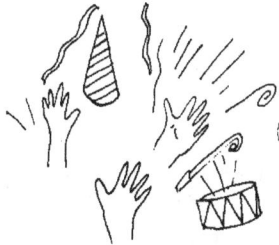

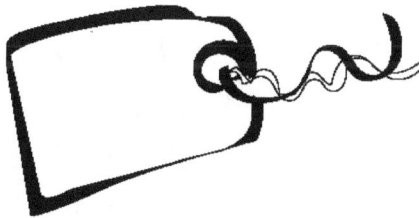

FIND THE LETTER

G	DUG	RUN	SWUM
R	RUT	SUM	FUR
M	GUST	MUST	DUST
D	RUST	MUG	DUST
U	GUN	NAN	GUS
N	NUT	RUST	RUN
T	GUN	RUT	TUG
S	FAN	SUN	DUST

MATCHING WORDS

DRUM	FUN
FUN	TRUST
GUM	DRUM
MUST	US
RUN	GUM
SUN	MUST
TRUST	RUN
US	SUN

FINDING WORDS/READING ALOUD

DRUM	DRUM	FUR	RUT
FUN	ADD	FUN	RUN
NUT	MUD	MUD	ANT
RUG	FUR	SUM	RUG
RUT	GUN	GUN	TUG
MUST	NUT	MAD	NUT
DAN	RUN	RUN	FUR
SUN	RUT	RUN	SUN
FUR	NUT	DUST	DUST
MUST	RUT	TUG	MUST

FLASH IDENTIFICATION

MUST	NUT	DUST	MAD
MAST	MUD	SAM	FUN
AS	SWUM	SUN	MUD
WAS	FUN	FAR	AS
FUR	TUG	FAR	SUM
SUM	DAN	SWAN	RAT
RUG	DUG	MUM	TUG
FAR	MUD	MAM	SAM

SOUNDS IN WORDS

DRAM	DAM	MUTT	DARTS
GUST	DUST	RAG	ANT
SAND	NUT	RUST	AS
MAN	SUM	RAW	SWUM
DRUM	SUN	RUN	US
MUST	DUST	TUG	RAN
SWAM	DUG	WARD	AN
NAN	WANT	TAN	TRUST
SAND	RAFT	MAN	MAD
TAR	RAN	WANT	SAT

DICTATION

_____

- -

- -

HOW MANY WORDS CAN YOU MAKE
G, S, T, N, U, D, R

WHAT IS THIS?   CAN YOU MAKE IT BETTER?

CAN YOU DRAW IT BETTER DOWN HERE?

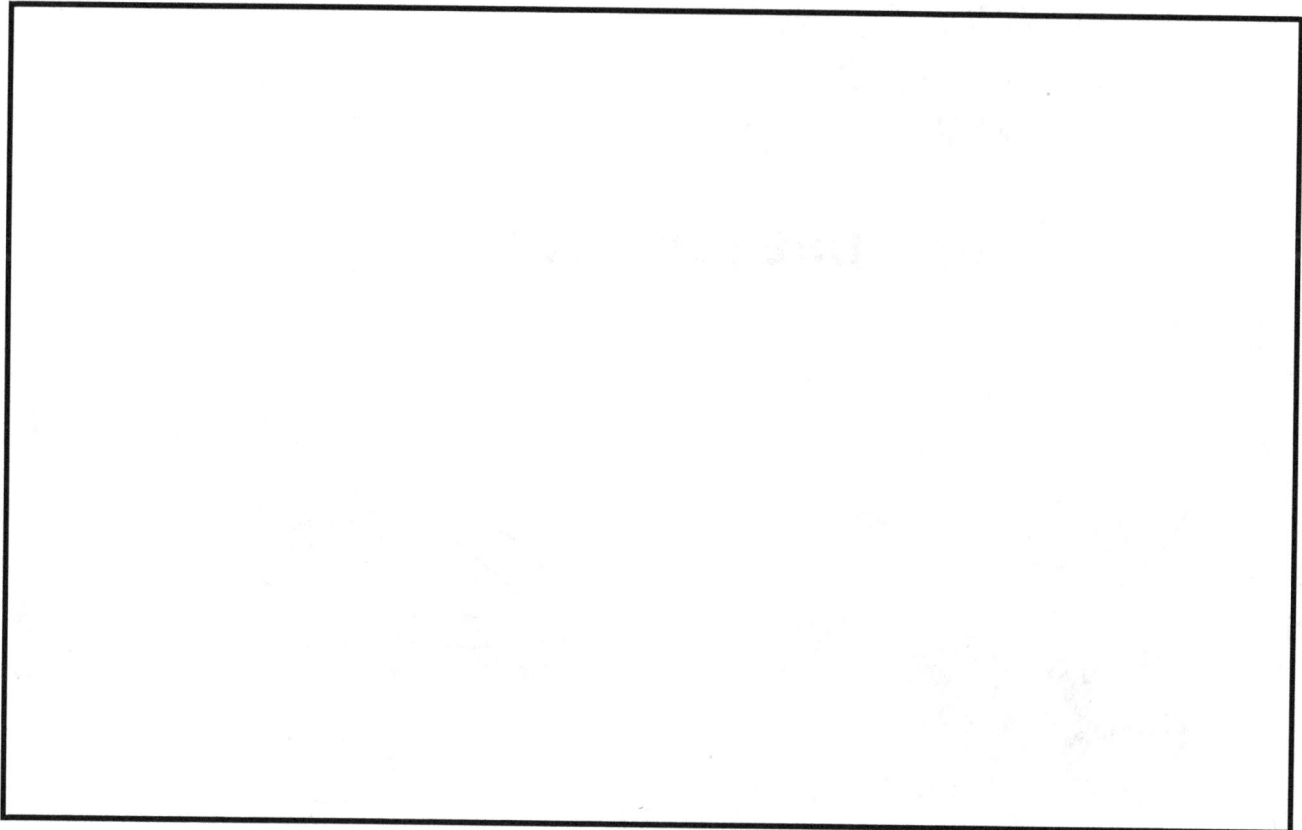

Professor Bloomer's No-Nonsense Reading Program
Lesson 11

PHRASES TO COPY AND READ ALOUD

NAN SAW A DRUM._____

DAN SAW A GUN. _____

A RAT MUST RUN FAST. _____

DAN SAW NAN DUST A MUG. _____

SAM MUST TUG AND DRAG A RAFT. _____

A FARM WAS FUN. _____

A RAT DUG A NUT. _____

DAD SAW US RUN FAST. _____

DAN MUST DUST A RUG._____

COMPLETING SENTENCES

SAM M__ST RUN FAST.

DAN SAW A G__N.

DAD SAW US R__N F__ST.

A F__RM WAS F__N.

PICTURE PHRASES

PICTURE PHRASES

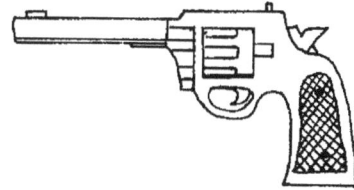

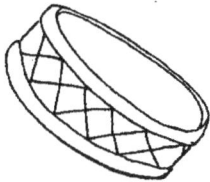

H

_____

_____

PICTURES TO LABEL

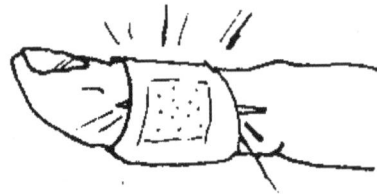

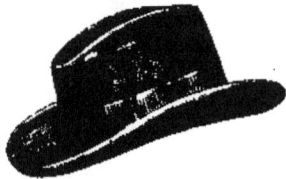

MATCH AND LABEL

HAM
HAT
HUT
HAND
HURT
FARM
DRUM
HARD
NUT
HAMMERS

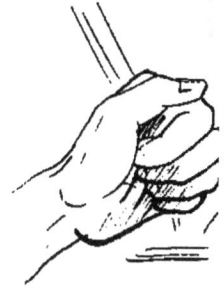

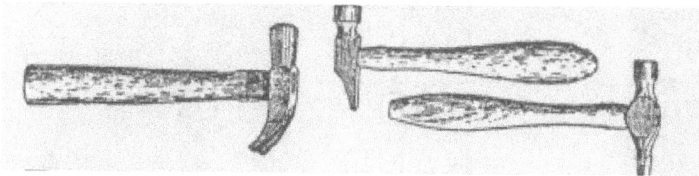

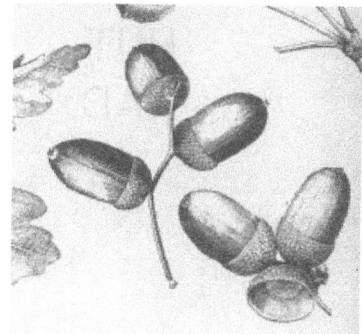

FIND THE LETTER

H	HAM	SAD	WARM
M	SAM	HAM	HAD
N	HAND	FAR	HARM
D	HAD	HARD	HUM
H	STAR	HARM	HAT
R	HURT	AS	HAS
T	HAND	HUT	RAM
H	HAD	TAR	SAT

MATCHING WORDS

HAM	HUT
HARD	HAM
HURT	HUG
HUG	HARD
HAS	HAS
HAND	HAD
HUT	HAND
HAD	HURT

FINDING WORDS/READING ALOUD

HURT	HUT	HAD	HURT
HAM	HAND	HAND	HARM
HAD	HURT	HAD	HAS
HUM	HARD	HARD	HAT
HAND	HAM	HURT	HAM
HUT	HAD	HUT	HAS
HUM	HUM	HAND	HARD
HAS	HURT	HARM	HARM
HUG	HAM	HUG	HAD
HAD	HAS	HAS	HAND

FLASH IDENTIFICATION

HARM	HAD	MAD	RAW
FARM	HARM	HAT	DUG
SUM	SUN	HARM	HAND
HUM	HUT	HAT	HAM
FAT	HAS	FAST	HAT
FAN	NUT	HARD	DART
HUT	HURT	HAD	HUM
FAST	HAD	MAD	TAD

SOUNDS IN WORDS

AND	HAD	DUST	HUM	DART
DUN	HUG	MAST	FUN	SAND
RAN	HAD	GUST	HAND	NUT
DAD	HURT	HARM	SWAM	HAM
HAM	MAN	DRAG	HAND	GUN
HAT	SAD	HURT	HARM	DUG
WAS	HAS	HUM	NUT	HUT
RAN	SAW	DRAM	HAS	AND

DICTATION

HOW MANY WORDS CAN YOU MAKE
H, A, N, U, R, D, S, T

WHAT IS THIS?   CAN YOU MAKE IT BETTER?

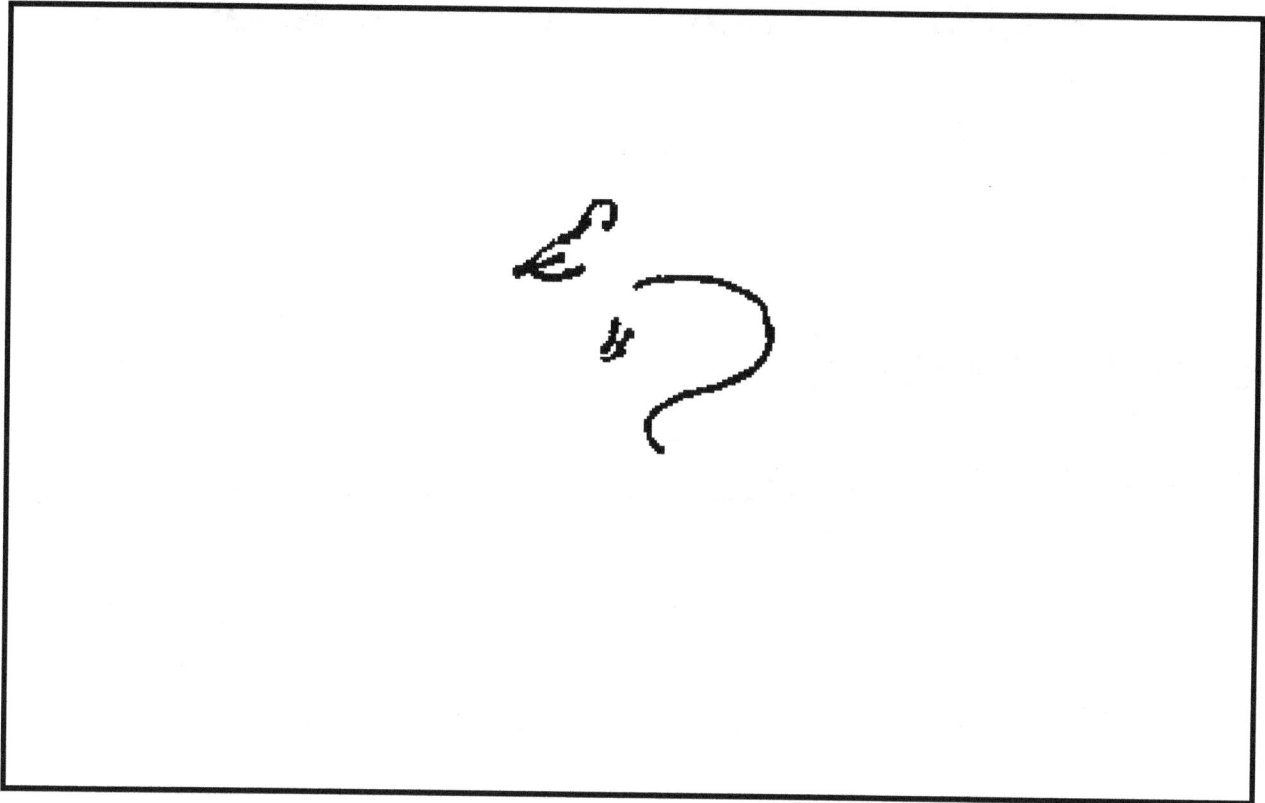

CAN YOU DRAW IT BETTER DOWN HERE?

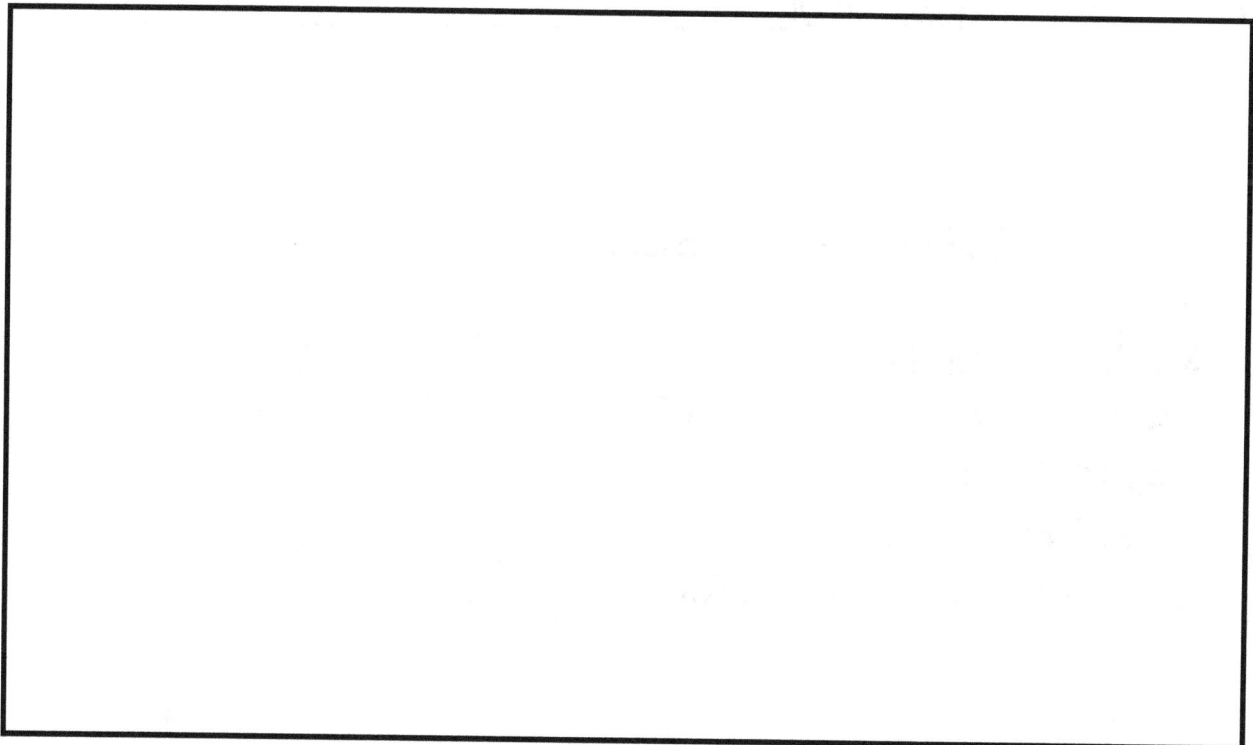

PHRASES TO COPY AND READ ALOUD

A RAT HAD A HAM._____

RUST HURTS A GUN_____

A RAT HAS TAN FUR_____

DAN HAD A HURT HAND_____

DADS HAT WAS MUD AND DUST_____

MAMA HUGS SAM_____

HARD TAR HURT NAN_____

A RAM CAN HARM SAM_____

COMPLETING SENTENCES

A RAT __AS TAN FUR.
DAN'S __AND __AS HURT.
MAMA H__GS SAM.
A RAT HAD A H__M.
A RAM CAN __ARM SAM.

PICTURE PHRASES

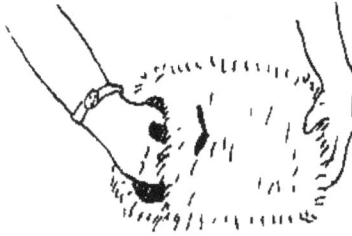

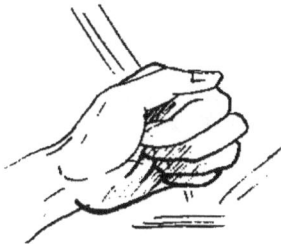

J_____

_____

PICTURES TO LABEL

MATCH AND LABEL

JAM
HATS
JUG
HUG
HUT
JAG
JAW
WAR
JAR
GUST

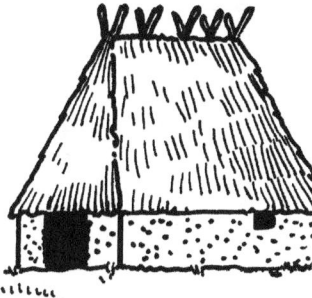

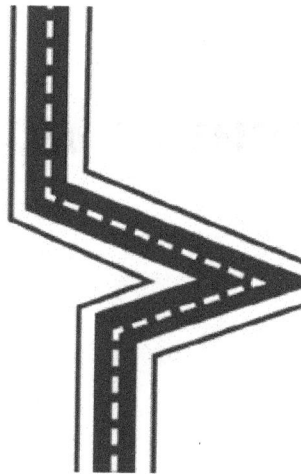

FIND THE LETTER

J	JAR	SAM	JAN
N	STAR	FAR	NUT
A	MUD	JAM	SAT
W	JAW	TUG	WAG
T	RUT	NAN	JUT
J	JUST	DAM	MUST
U	MAD	JUG	ART
R	JAR	DAN	RUN

MATCHING WORDS

JUT	JAM
JAM	JAW
JAR	JUT
JAW	JUST
JUST	JAN
JAN	JAR

FINDING WORDS/READING ALOUD

JAW	MAT	JAW	JUST
JUT	JUG	JUG	JAM
JUST	SAM	JUG	JUST
JUT	JUT	RUT	JUG
JAG	JAM	JAN	JAG
JUST	JAG	JAN	JAN
JAR	JUT	JAR	HAM
JAW	JAM	JAM	JAR

FLASH IDENTIFICATION

HAM	FAN	JAM	HARM
RUST	JUST	MUST	DUST
GAS	JAR	JUG	DART
JUT	MAT	HUT	TAD
FAN	JAW	RAW	JAN
JAM	JAR	JAN	JAW
JAM	FAN	FAT	JAN
JUT	DRAG	JUG	HAD

SOUNDS IN WORDS

MAD	JAM	DRAM	WAS
JAW	FAD	GRASS	ADD
JAM	WART	MAD	TAD
JAW	WAG	ADD	WART
FAD	SAW	MAD	RAFT
DAM	GAS	JAR	SAW
MAD	JAR	RAM	SAT
SAD	FAST	JAR	WAS

DICTATION

HOW MANY WORDS CAN YOU MAKE?
J, U, A, S, T, M, R, H

WHAT IS THIS?   CAN YOU MAKE IT BETTER?

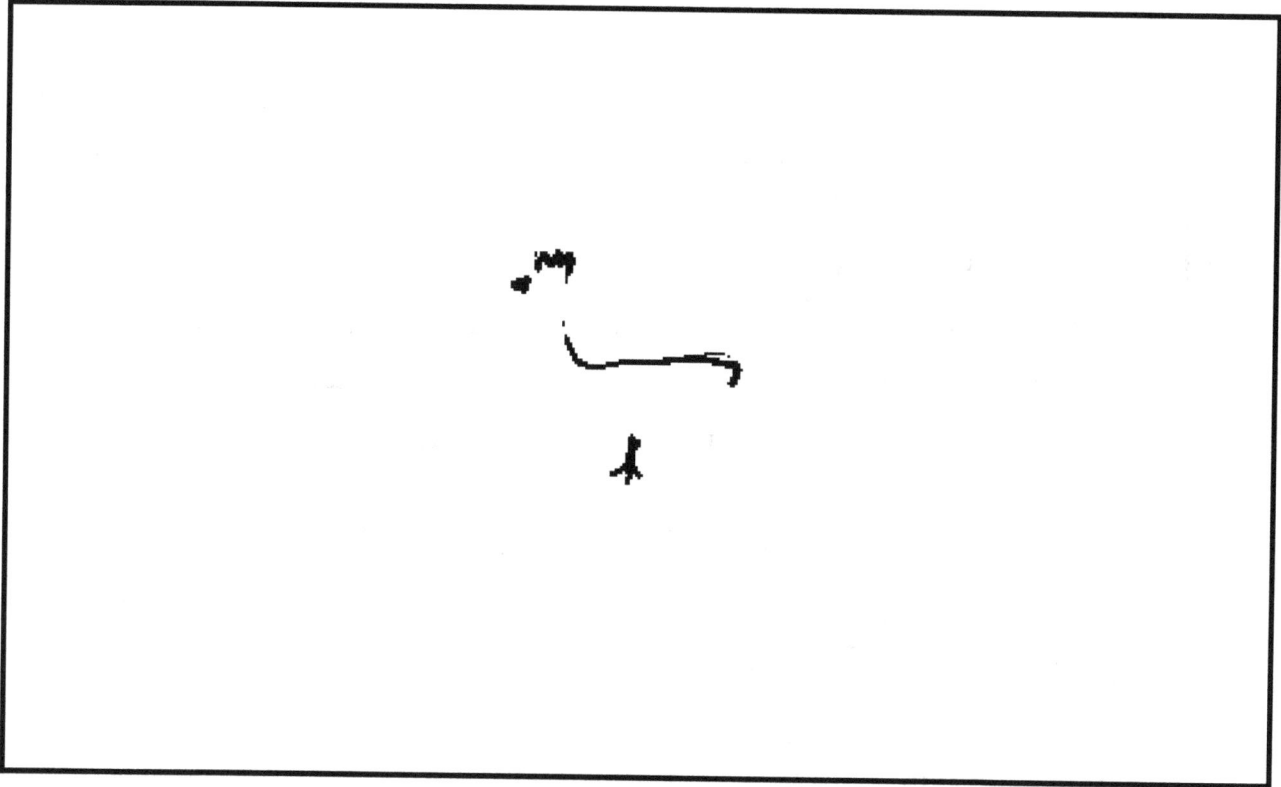

CAN YOU DRAW IT BETTER DOWN HERE?

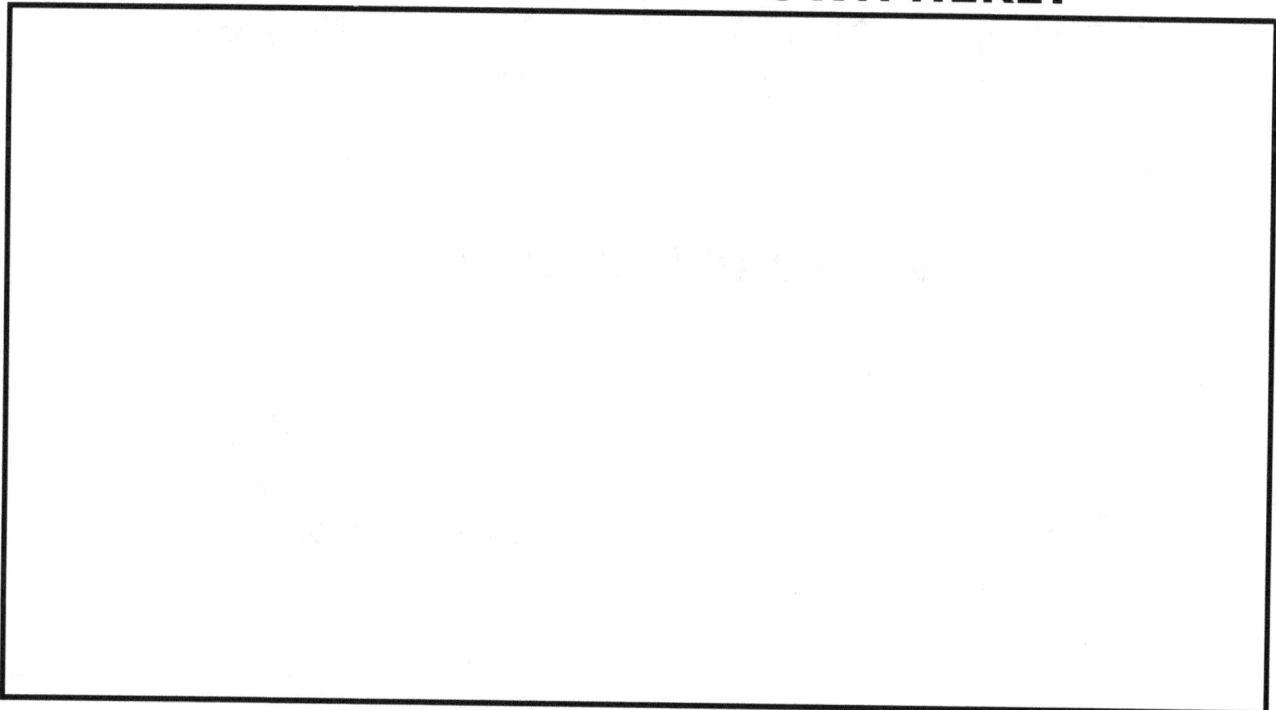

PHRASES TO COPY AND READING ALOUD

AN ANT SAT AT A JAM JAR._____

JAN DUSTS A JUG._____

A RAT JUST HAD A JAM TART._____

A HARD JUT HURT SAM'S JAW._____

A RAT SAT AT A JAM JAR._____

JAM SAW A JAM JAR._____

JAN JUST RAN AND RAN FAST._____

COMPLETING SENTENCES

JAN D_STS A JU_.

A RAT __UST HAD A JAM TART.

SAM HAS A __UG.

SAM WANTS A __AM JAR.

NAN __UST HAD A J___M TART.

HOW MANY SENTENCES CAN YOU MAKE?

GLASS, LAD, FULL, LAST, SAM, FAST, HAD, DUG, A, GLAD, FALL, JUST, AND, HAS, NAN, TALL.

PICTURE PHRASES

PICTURE PHRASES

L

PICTURES TO LABEL

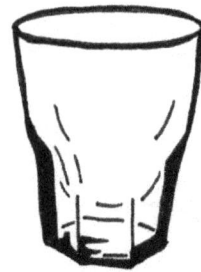

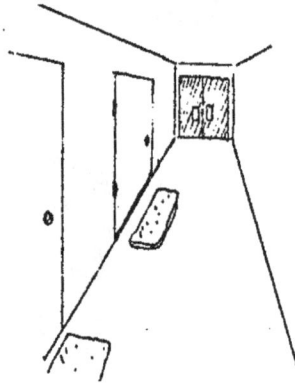

MATCH AND LABEL

FLAG
LUGS
RUG
JUG
FALL
LAND
HULL
SALT
GULL
SALAD
GLASS

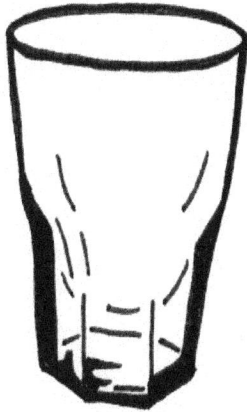

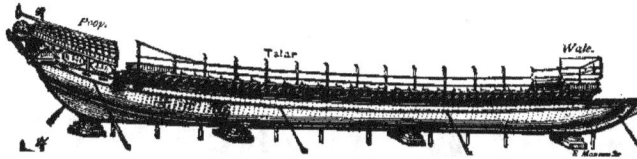

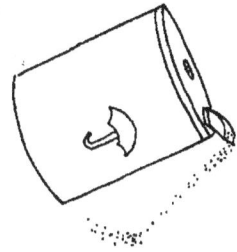

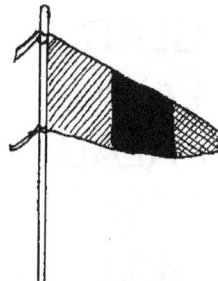

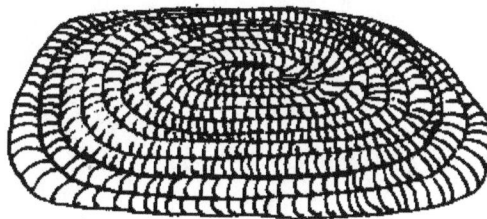

MATCHING WORDS

LARD	GLASS
GLASS	DULL
LAD	LAND
SLAM	LAD
DULL	SLAM
LUG	LARD
LAND	GLAD
GLAD	LUG

FINDING THE WORD/READING ALOUD

GLASS	LAW	GLASS	LAG
LAW	LAD	LAD	DULL
LARD	LASS	GLAD	LASS
GLAD	GLAD	LAG	LAND
GLASS	ALAS	ALAS	LAW
SLAM	LAG	LASS	SLAM
LAND	GLAD	LAG	LAG
LAW	LAW	GLASS	GLAD
LAG	SALAD	LAND	SALAD
DULL	LASS	DULL	LARD
LAW	GULL	GULL	GLASS

FLASH IDENTIFICATION

WALL	WAR	LAD	HAD
HARD	LAG	LARD	RAG
FLAG	FAST	LAST	GLAD
HUM	TALL	FULL	DULL
LAND	HAND	JAM	HALL
LUG	GLASS	JUG	LASS
FLAT	TAG	LAG	SALAD
HAD	LAW	JAW	HUG

SOUNDS IN WORDS

HAM	ALAS	FAT	DULL	FALL
LULL	SALAD	SLAT	TALL	LUG
SANTA	HALL	HULL	WALL	LAND
SLAG	GRASS	TAGGED	FLAT	LAST
TALL	FLAT	JAM	HUMMED	FURRED
GLASS	LAND	FLAG	SUMMED	NUT
SALAD	GULL	GLAD	WALL	FALL
FALSE	HULL	GLASS	SLAT	LAD

DICTATION

WHAT IS THIS? CAN YOU MAKE IT BETTER?

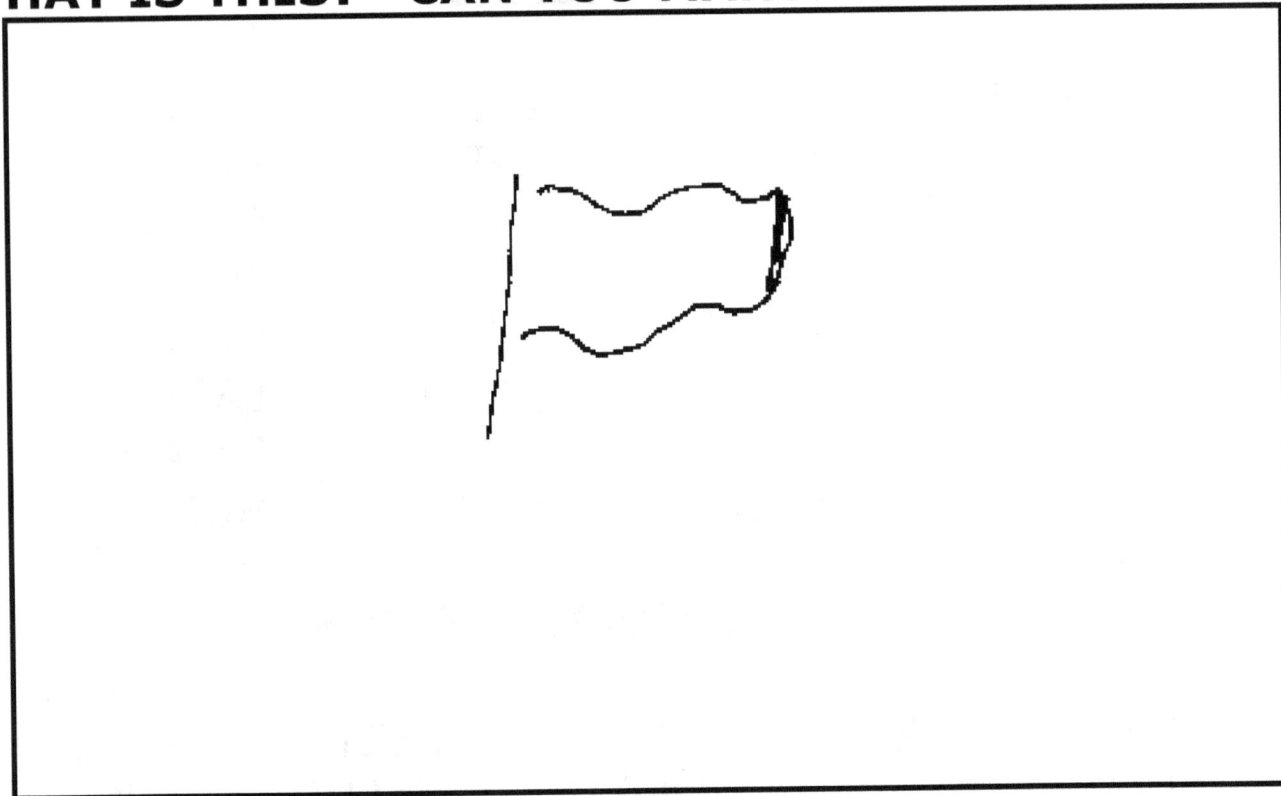

CAN YOU DRAW IT BETTER DOWN HERE?

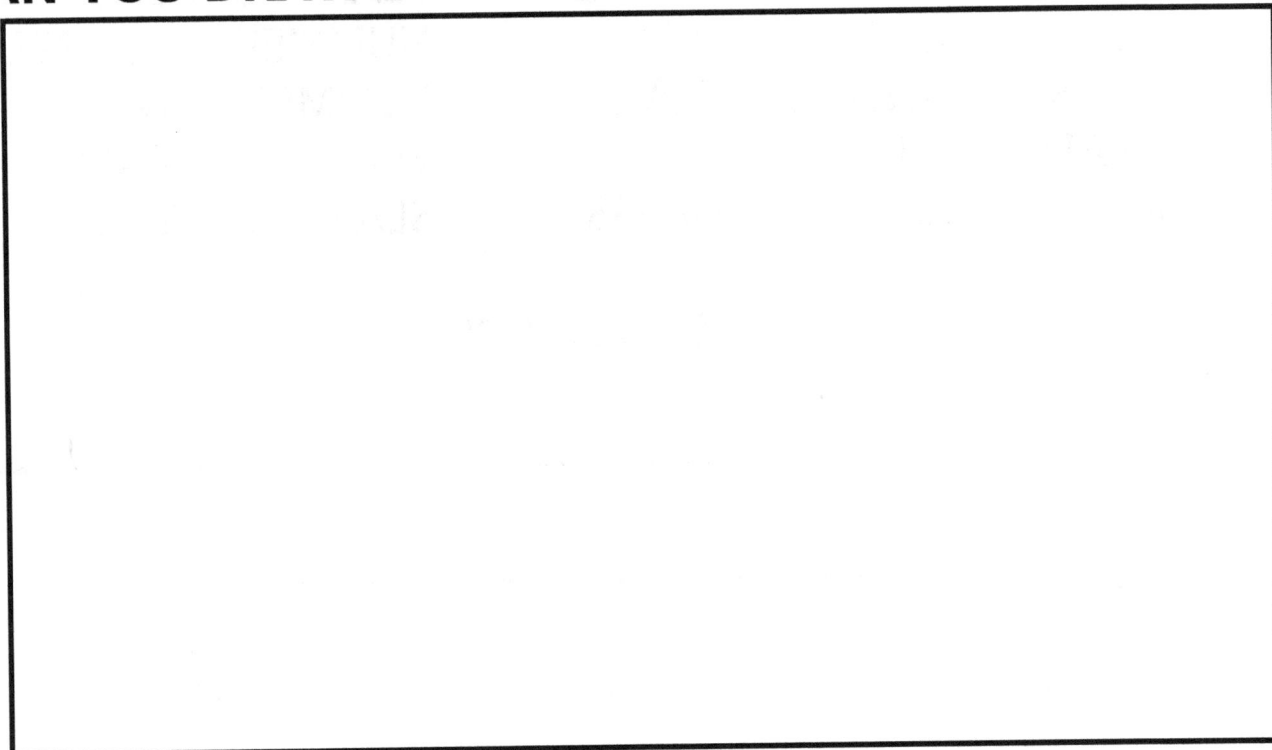

HOW MANY WORDS CAN YOU MAKE?
L, R, A, F, U, M, T, S, G, H.

PHRASES TO COPY AND READ ALOUD

A LAD AND A LASS RAN FAST._____

_____

A LAD HAD A SALAD AND WAS FULL._____

_____

NAN AND DAN HAD A FLAG._____

_____

GLASS WALL WAS DULL._____

_____

A FLAT RAFT HAD A TALL MAST._____

_____

MORE PHRASES TO COPY AND READ ALOUD

A GULL TUGGED AT A TART._____

_____

MAMA AND DAD WERE GLAD._____

_____

DAN WAS FULL AT LAST._____

_____

A TALL LAD DUG GRASS_____

_____

COMPLETING SENTENCES

A FLAT RA__T HAD A TA__ MAST.
A __AD HAD A SA__AD.
DAN RAN L__ST.
A FARM HAD __ARD __AND.
DAN HAD A FLA__.

\

PICTURE PHRASES

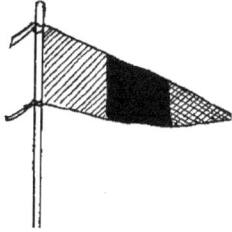

HOW MANY SENTENCES CAN YOU MAKE?

GLASS, LAD, FULL, LAST, SAM, FAST, HAD, DUG, A, GLAD, FALL, JUST, AND, HAS, NAN, TALL, WAS, SAW,

C _____

_____

PICTURES TO LABEL

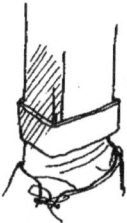

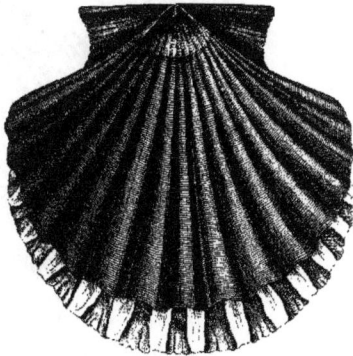

MATCH AND LABEL

CAT
CAN
CARD
CAR
CRAG
DRAG
SCAN
CUT
CART
CLAM

MATCHING WORDS

CAN	CAT
CAR	CAN
SCAN	CARD
CRAM	CRAM
CAT	CAR
CARD	SCAN
CAW	CRAFT
CRAFT	CAW

FIND THE WORD/READING ALOUD

CAN	CAR	LAND	CAR
SCAN	SCAN	CAN	CRAM
CAN	LARD	CAN	HAM
CALL	CRAM	CRAM	SCRAM
CULL	CAR	CURD	CULL
CAD	CUR	CUR	CARD
SCAN	CAW	CALL	CAW
CARD	CUD	CARD	CRAM
CAR	CAT	CAT	SCAN
CURD	LAD	CALL	CURD

FLASH IDENTIFICATION

CART	GUST	DART	CRUST
CAT	CARD	CRAG	GAS
HAD	CAST	CAR	TAR
GUST	DRAG	ACT	CRAG
DAN	CAN	CARD	GUST
FAST	CURL	CAST	LAST
CURD	CALL	CURL	CRAG
CAT	CRAM	SAT	GAS

SOUNDS IN WORDS

HAD	CRAM	DART	CUT	CART
CAR	CURD	LAST	DAN	DRUM
GIVE	RAG	CAST	CURT	FALL
CUR	LAD	HAS	CAT	SLAM
HAD	HULL	CAT	JAG	LAND
SAT	HAND	MAST	CAN	CRAG

DICTATION

WHAT IS THIS?   CAN YOU MAKE IT BETTER?

CAN YOU DRAW IT BETTER DOWN HERE?

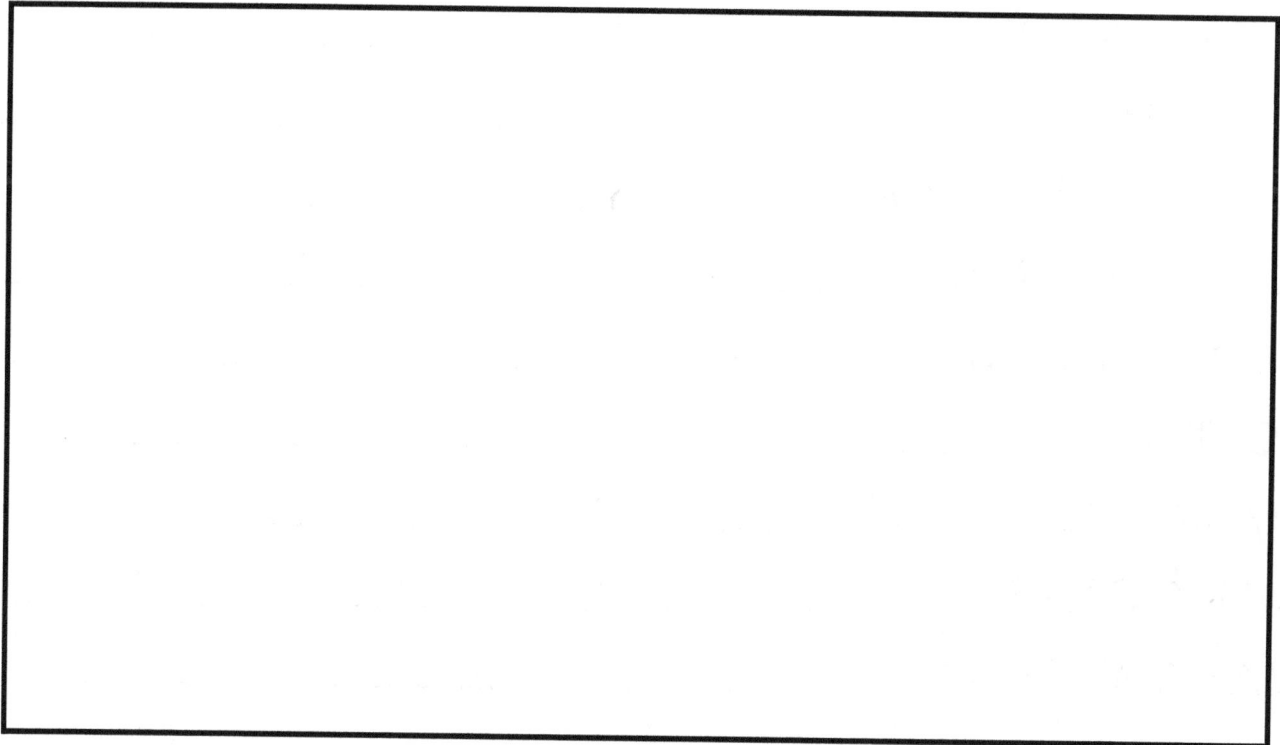

HOW MANY WORDS CAN YOU MAKE?
C, N, A, T, R, U, M, D, G

PHRASES TO COPY AND READ ALOUD

A CUB DUG MUD AND DUST._____

A CUB RAN UP A CRAG._____

A CAR CAN RUN FAST._____

A CAR HAS GAS._____

A CAR CAN RUST_____

A CAT SAT ON A CRAG. _____

A RAT HAD A CRUST._____

A CAT CAN HURT A RAT._____

A RAT CAN RUN._____

SAM CAN DRAW A CAT_____

SCAT, CAT._____

MAMA HAD A CARD._____

MAMA CALLS JAN._____

MAMA WAS CURT._____

COMPLETING SENTENCES

DAN C_N'T CU_   A CAN.
SAM CAN D_AW A   C_T
A CAT CA_   HURT A RAT
A CAT _AN R_N FAST.
_N ANT CRAWLS AT A C_N
 A CAT D_G MUD.

PICTURE PHRASES

PICTURE PHRASES

HOW MANY SENTENCES CAN YOU MAKE?

CAT SAND A DUG RUN SAT CAN
CALL JAN CAN'T AND CARD SCAT DAN

PICTURES TO LABEL

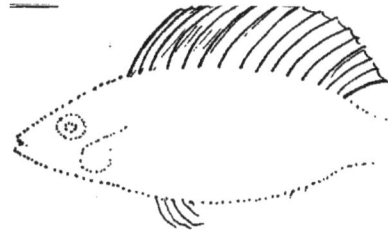

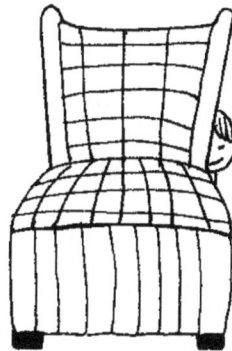

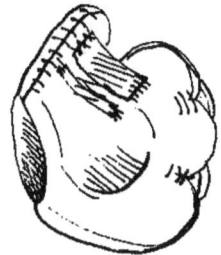

MATCH AND LABEL

MILL
MISS
HIT
MIT
GIRL
SING
FIG
FIN
GIFT
LID

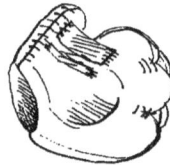

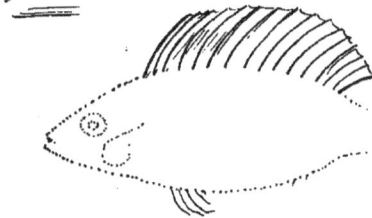

MATCHING WORDS

WIN	DIM
JILL	SWIM
SING	MISS
FIRM	IS
SWIM	GIRL
DIG	WIN
DIM	FIRM
IS	DIG
MISS	SING
GIRL	JILL

FINDING WORDS/READING WORDS ALOUD

FIRM	SWIM	WIN	SWIM
IF	FIN	JIM	IF
IS	SIS	SIS	RINSE
DID	DID	FIG	WIN
LID	MISS	GIVE	GIVE
RINSE	FIN	FIN	TAR
IN	JIG	IN	JIM
RIM	FIG	FIG	CARD
DID	IS	IS	SAT
JIM	CURT	JIM	DIM
RINSE	RINSE	FIG	RISK

FLASH IDENTIFICATION

DAD	DID	LAD	AMID
SATIN	DIRT	IT	SLAM
FIT	HID	HIT	SIT
LITTLE	FIN	FAN	FLAT
HID	HILL	LAD	FALL
HILL	DIRT	DART	HALT
GIFT	ILL	TIN	DAN
HAS	HIS	LAST	LIST

SOUNDS IN WORDS

GIG	CAST	LIMIT	SLAT	HILL
RIM	FIT	LIST	FAN	MIST
LARD	DARE	MILL	HIM	LIST
VAST	WIG	HAD	SWAM	SWIM
SLIM	TRIM	JIM	RIG	JAW
DIM	DRAM	FIST	RINSE	TIM
FIG	WIN	LID	MISS	GIVE
IS	SAT	JIM	CURT	DIM

DICTATION

_____

_____

_____

WHAT IS THIS?   CAN YOU MAKE IT BETTER?

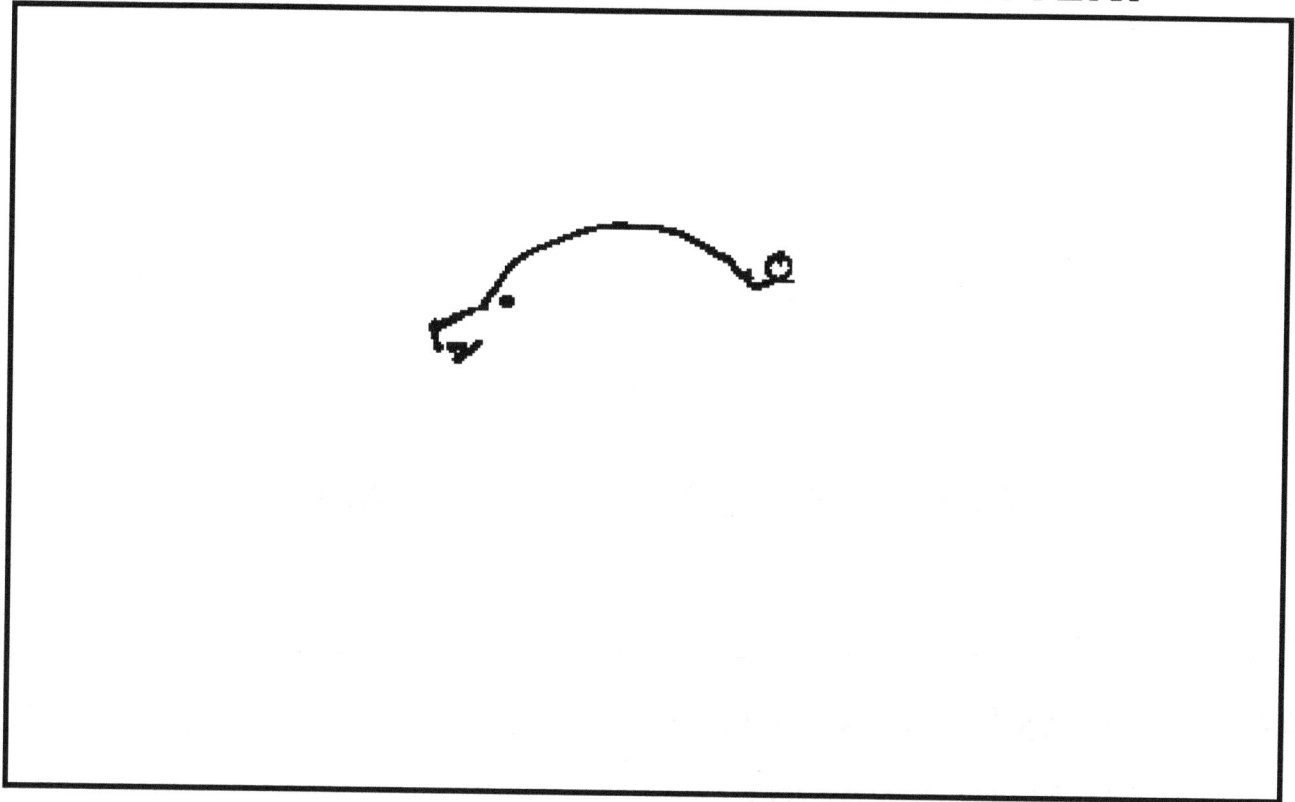

CAN YOU DRAW IT BETTER DOWN HERE?

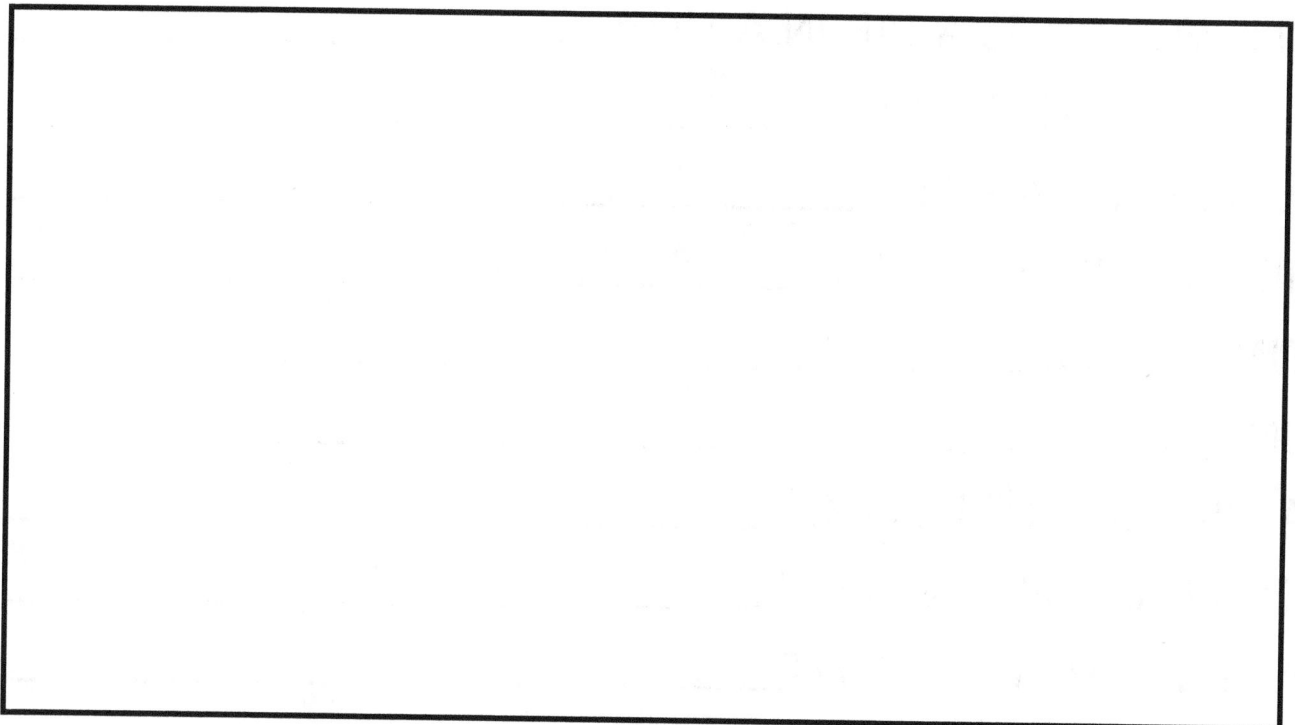

HOW MANY WORDS CAN YOU MAKE
I. W, M. S, R. T. L, N, D, A

PHRASES TO COPY AND READ ALOUD

A RAT RAN IN A MILL._____

AN ANT WAS IN A SAND HILL._____

AN ANT WAS IN A SALAD._____

JILL IS A GIRL._____

JILL WILL RINSE A JAR IN A SINK._____

JILL MUST RUN A HILL._____

A MIST HID A HILL._____

JILL WILL WIN AT TAG._____

TIM HIT JIM._____

JIM IS IN A FIT._____

A FIST HIT LITTLE TIM._____

JIM WILL GIVE TIM A WIG._____

A MAN'S HAT MUST FIT_____

COMPLETING SENTENCES

J_M AND SIS H_D A GIFT.
TIM W_LL VISIT SAM.
A _AN'S HAT MUST F_T.
A CAN _S T_N.
DAN WAS ILL IN A W_RD.
A RAT CAN R_N _N A M_LL.
A CAT CAN D__G IN SAND.
__N ANT SAT __N A JAM J__R LID.

PICTURE PHRASES

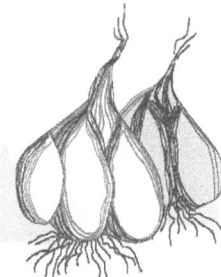

HOW MANY SENTENCES CAN YOU MAKE?
CAN, MAN, MILL, ANT, HURT, HAD, HAT, HAS, GULL, DIRT, IN, HULL, HIS, FIT, AN, SWIM, A, NAN, JUST, RAN, AND, WAS, SAW IN.

V _____

_____

PICTURES TO LABEL

MATCH AND LABEL

VAT
MAT
LAVA
VISIT
VAN
MAN
VAST
MAST
LIST
FIST
FAN
SWIM

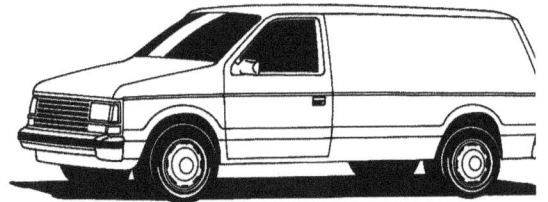

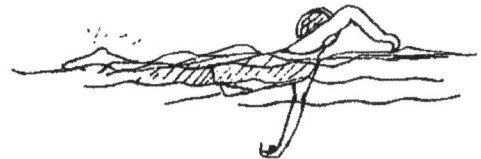

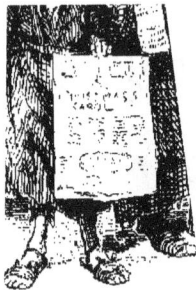

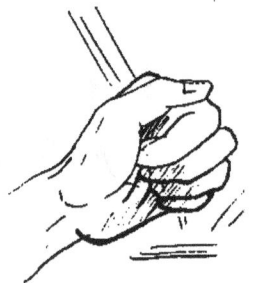

MATCHING WORDS

VISIT	LAVA
HAVE	HAVE
LAVA	VAST
VISTA	VAT
VAT	VISIT
VAST	VISTA

FINDING THE WORD/READ ALOUD

HAVE	HAVE	VISIT	VAT
VISTA	LAVA	VAST	LAVA
HAVE	VAST	VAST	VISIT
VISTA	LAVA	VISIT	VISTA
VAST	VAT	HAVE	VAT
LAVA	VAT	VISIT	VISIT

FLASH IDENTIFICATION

HAVE	MAT	VAST	VISIT
VAST	FAT	VAT	FIRST
VAST	MIST	MAST	VISIT
FARM	WAS	CAT	VAST
LAVA	VAT	HAD	NAT
SAW	RAM	VAN	RAW
WARM	VAN	MAN	NAT
VAST	MAST	VAT	WAS

SOUNDS IN WORDS

SLAT	LAVA	HARM	VAT	LUG
MUST	DRUM	FLAT	LAVA	HARM
DUB	SWAN	SUM	FLAG	VAN
HARE	GLASS	HAVE	SWUM	US
VAN	SLAG	LAST	VAST	MUST
LAVA	VAST	ALUM	SWAM	LARD
ALUM	SLAM	DRAG	LAVA	HARD

DICTATION

HOW MANY WORDS CAN YOU MAKE?
V, L, A, H, I, S, T, N, R

WHAT IS THIS?   CAN YOU MAKE IT BETTER?

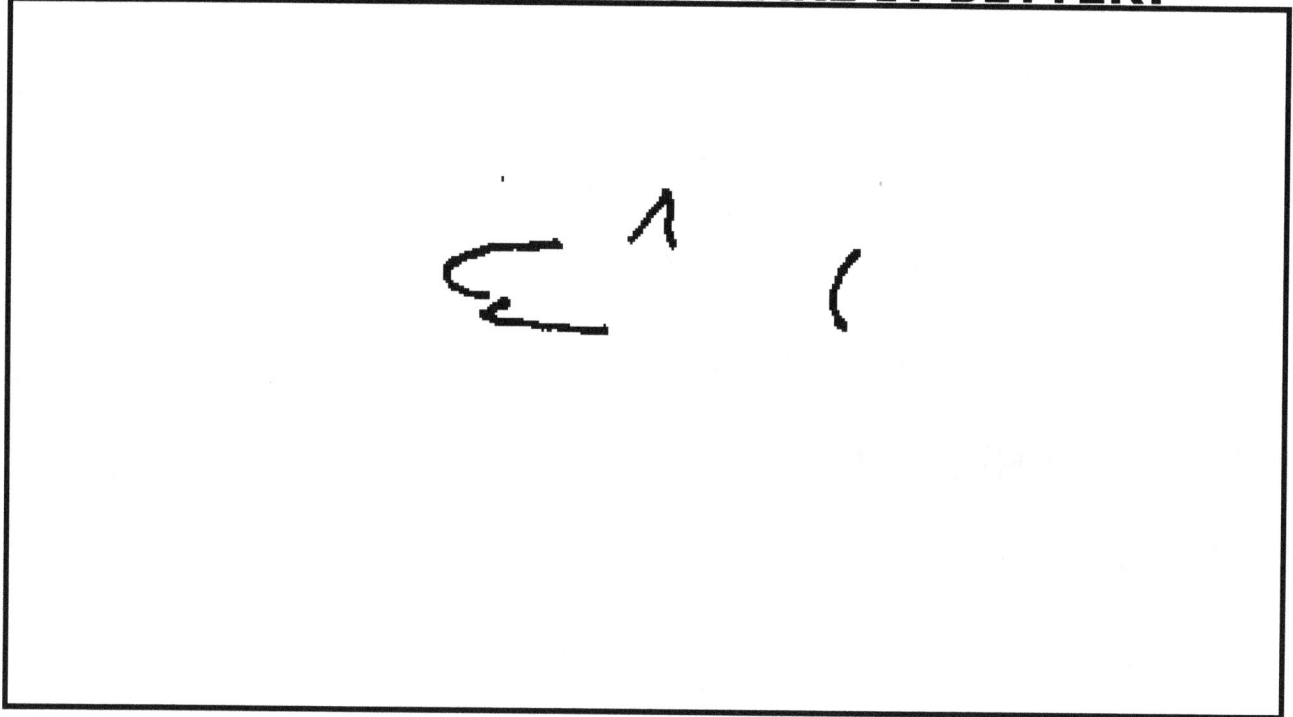

CAN YOU DRAW IT BETTER DOWN HERE?

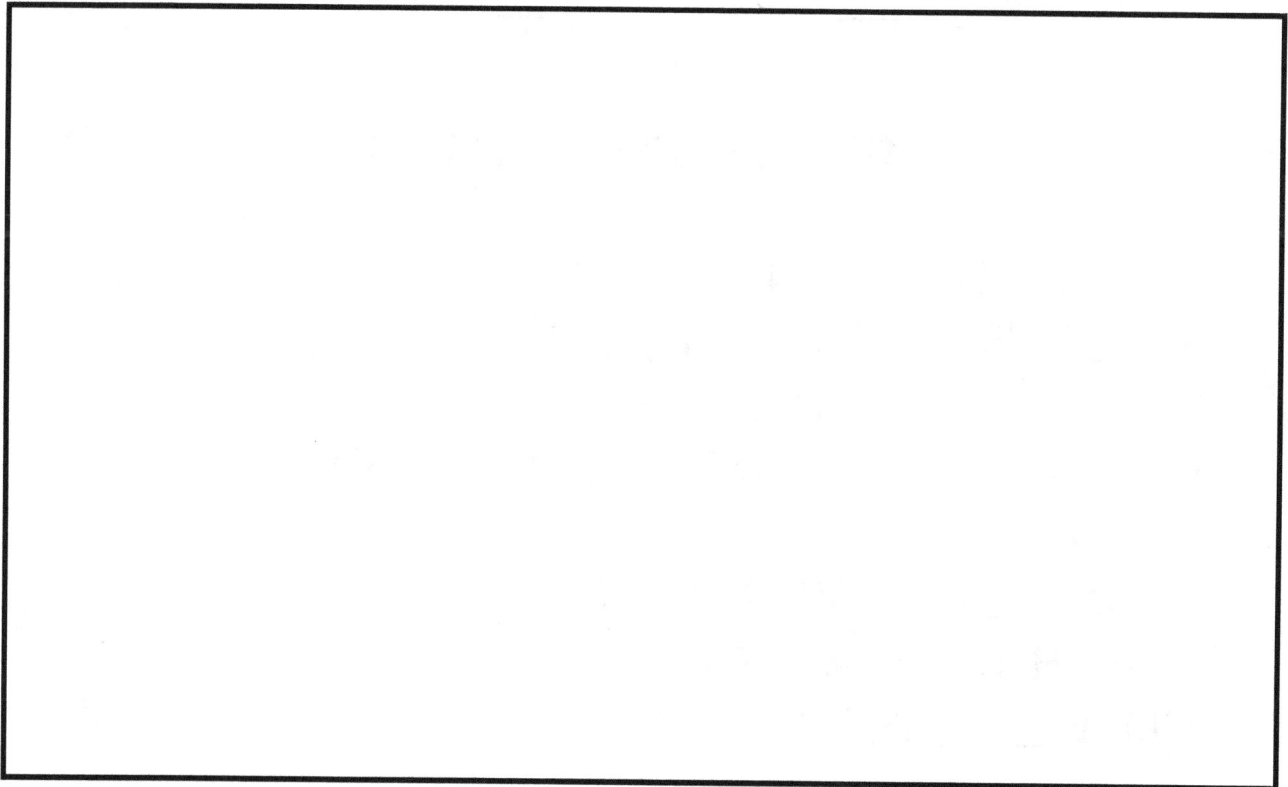

PHRASES TO COPY AND READ ALOUD

JIM AND SIS HAVE A GIFT._____

MAMA AND DAD HAVE A FLAG._____

A VAST LAND WAS DUST AND SAND._____

RATS AND CATS HAVE FUN._____

A FULL VAN HAD A FLAT._____

A VAT WILL FILL A JUG._____

IF DAN CALLS TIM WILL VISIT HIM._____

A VAN WILL RUN ON FIRM DIRT._____

SAM IS IN A VAT._____

COMPLETING SENTENCES

A VAN SAN__ IN THE MUD.
A __AN'S HAT MUST __IT.
JACK HAS A HAR__ TASK.
JAN WILL ASK SANTA __OR A GI__T.
A CAT _AN SWI_.
A FULL _AN HAD A FLAT.
SAM H_D IN A _AT.
TIM W__LL VIS_T SAM.

PICTURE PHRASES

HOW MANY SENTENCES CAN YOU MAKE?

CAT	HAVE	AND	CAN	TIN
A	SAM	VAT	RAT	IS
VAN	FUN	VISIT	RUN	SWIM
NAN	VISTA	SAW	AND	AT

K

PICTURES TO LABEL

MILK

IN

MATCH AND LABEL

SKIRT
SINK
INK
HIT
DUCKS
DOCK
KICK
TACK
TRUNK
MILK
WALK
SACK

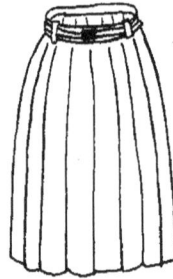

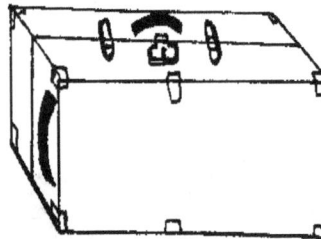

MATCHING WORDS

INK	JUNK
JACK	ASK
ASK	JACK
TUCK	DICK
DARK	INK
DICK	DARK
JUNK	LICK
LICK	TUCK

FINDING WORDS/READING ALOUD

WINK	ASK	DICK	WINK
CLACK	TACK	DARK	TACK
RANK	DICK	RANK	SINK
SKID	SLACK	INK	SLACK
TANK	TANK	RANK	RISK
ASK	SACK	SACK	DUST
TUCK	SAND	DANK	SANK
LICK	DUCK	DUCK	MARK
MASK	SKID	MASK	MUSK
SILK	MUSK	SINK	SINK

FLASH IDENTIFICATION

HICK	HID	KID	FAT
LAVA	MAD	WAR	MAN
KIT	FIT	HIT	FIRST
MAD	HUNK	KIT	HIT
INK	FIN	DRINK	VAT
LARK	RID	RUG	KID
DRAG	FARM	DRINK	HARD
DUSK	HIT	SKILL	HILL

SOUNDS IN WORDS

DUNK	DUCK	KICK	HAT	JAM
KINK	TACK	SACK	SINK	KID
DARK	ASK	SUNK	DRINK	DICK
VISIT	DUCK	INK	STACK	LUCK
TUCK	DIG	JACK	LICK	LIT
MASK	KISS	MARK	RINK	MINT
DUSK	DRAG	LARK	INK	HUNK
KIT	HIT	DRINK	FIN	INK
VAT	LARK	RID	RUG	KID

DICTATION

WHAT IS THIS? CAN YOU MAKE IT BETTER

CAN YOU MAKE IT EVEN BETTER HERE?

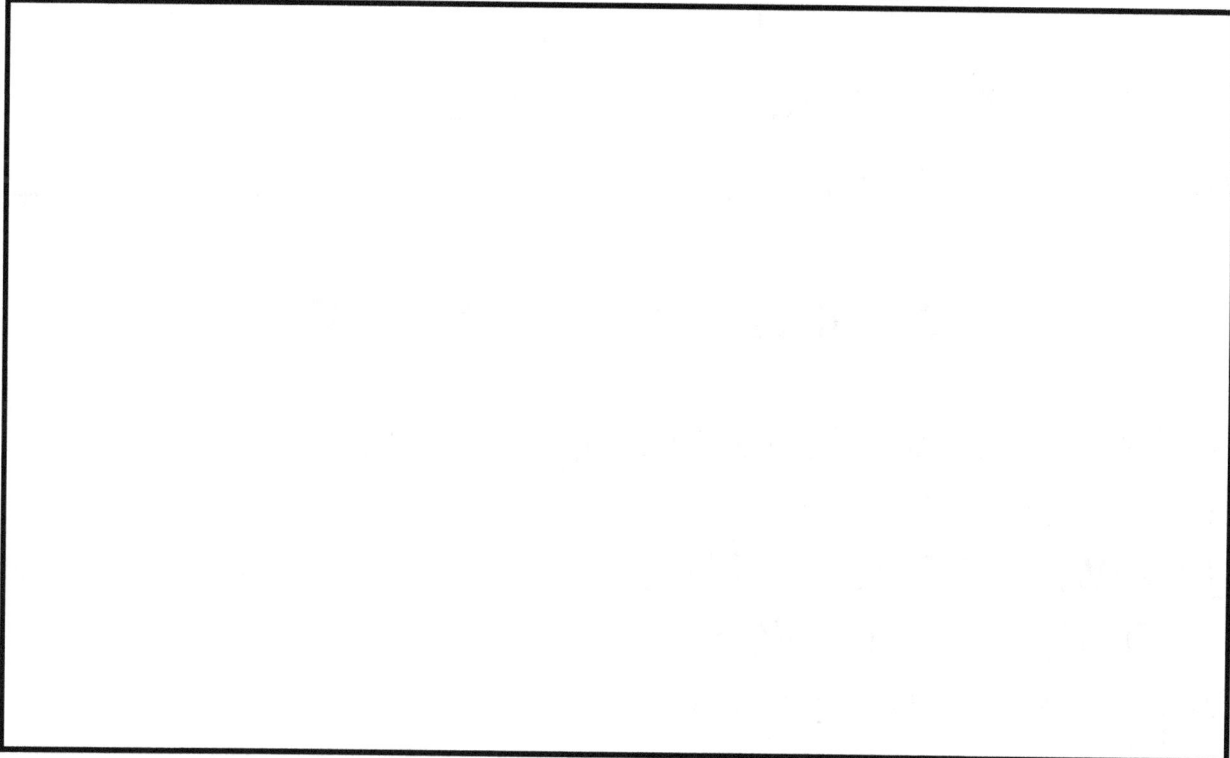

HOW MANY WORDS CAN YOU MAKE?
K, D, C, I, U, R, N, S, L

PHRASES TO COPY AND READ ALOUD

IT IS DARK IN A SACK._____

JILL WILL ASK SANTA._____

A DUCK CAN SWIM._____

JJACK HAS A HARD TASK._____

DAD HAD A TANK OF INK._____

SIS SAT ON A TACK._____

A CAT WILL LICK A KIT._____

A VAN SANK IN THE MUD._____

A CAT WILL DRINK MILK._____

A SWAN WILL SWIM AT DUSK._____

COMPLETING SENTENCES

JACK HAD A DARK MAS_.
DAN _AD A _ARD TAS_.
JAN WILL ACT AS_ SANT_.
A DUC_ _ _AN SW_M.
A CAT WI_ _ DR_NK MIL_.

PICTURE PHRASES

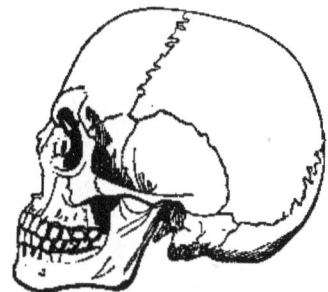

PICTURE PHRASES

HOW MANY SENTENCES CAN YOU MAKE?

CAN	ASK	LICK	MILL	A	LARK	JACK	SAW
CAT	DUNK	HAVE	IS	IN	VAT	VISTA	JILL
AND	AT	VISIT	HURT	SKULL	WAS	A	

B
_____

_____

PICTURES TO LABEL

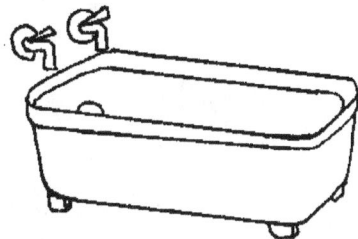

MATCH AND LABEL

BAT
BUS
DUCK
BUD
BARK
RABBIT
BIRD
BARN
CRAB
BUGS
BAT
BALL

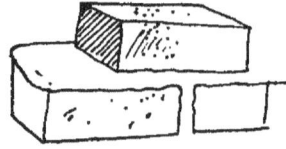

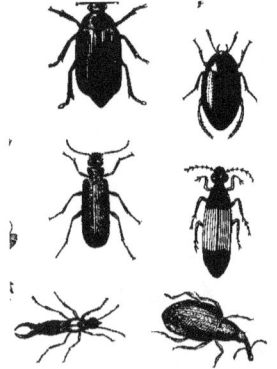

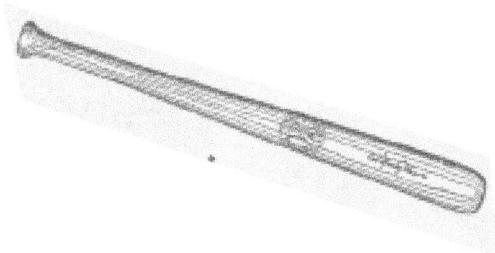

MATCHING WORDS

BAT	BUG
BUST	BAT
BUG	SLAB
BULL	BUST
CAB	JIB
RIB	CAB
JIB	RIB
SLAB	BULL

FINDING THE WORD/READING ALOUD

RABBIT	RABBIT	BASS	BRAG
BAT	BACK	BLAT	BACK
BAG	BUT	BUT	LAB
BULL	RIB	BUS	BULL
CAB	BANK	STUB	BANK
BLAST	BAT	BLAST	BRAN
RIB	BUST	BUG	BAG
BUN	BUNK	BUNK	BIN
BUG	BIG	BUG	BALL
BIRD	CUB	BIN	CUB

FLASH IDENTIFICATION

BIG	DIG	BAD	RAG
BUD	DULL	RAN	BULL
DUCK	BARN	BIG	RIG
BUST	DUST	BAND	RUST
BAD	BUST	GUST	BAG
TAR	TAG	TAB	BRAN
BARD	RABBIT	RAT	STAR
DUCK	BUNK	BID	KID

SOUNDS IN WORDS

FILL	MILL	RUB	BID	LID
BRASS	CAST	LIST	CAB	LIVE
CAT	SAW	BULB	BRIM	HURT
SLAM	RUB	CRAM	STUB	TUB
BUG	CART	BRAG	CURD	MINT
RINSE	CRAG	BASS	TRIM	BUG
DUCK	BARD	GUST	BRAN	STAR
BAD	BARN	DUST	BAND	RUST

DICTATION

WHAT IS THIS?   CAN YOU MAKE IT BETTER?

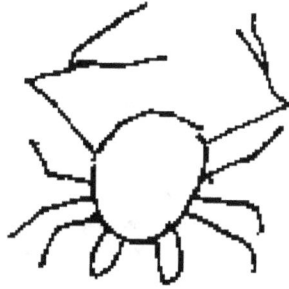

CAN YOU DRAW IT BETTER DOWN HERE?

HOW MANY WORDS CAN YOU MAKE?
B, R, A, C, S, G, T, I, L, N.

PHRASES TO COPY AND READ ALOUD

AN ANT BIT A MAN._____

BILL CAN BAT A BALL._____

AN ANT IS A BUG._____

A SWAN IS A BIG BIRD._____

BART HAS A BUN AND JAM._____

A BULL IS IN A BARN._____

A RABBIT RAN IN GRASS._____

A BIRD HAS A BILL._____

MAMA CAN RUB A GLASS._____

A FAT RAT WAS IN A BAG._____

A RAT WAS IN A BRAN BIN._____

THE HUT WAS IN A JUMBLE._____

A CAT SWAM IN A TUB._____

COMPLETING SENTENCES

BART HAS A _UN AND J_M.

AN ANT B_T MAMA.

BILL CAN _AT A _ALL.

DAN CAN D_G A _IG RUT.

MAMA _ILL FILL A G_ASS.

NAN WILL _UST A GLASS.

A RABBIT _ILL _UN IN G_ASS.

A B_LL IS IN A BARN.

PICTURE PHRASES

PICTURE PHRASES

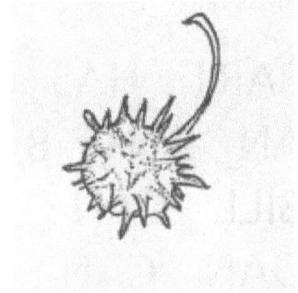

HOW MANY SENTENCES CAN YOU MAKE?

BAD	BILL	BUD	BUG	CAN	A	BUST
DIG	RUN	RABBIT	BIG	BULL	HAS	WAS
NAN	AND	BARN	WENT	IN	SWIM	RAN
UNDER	WAS	THE	UP	IT	IS	WANTS

O

_____

_____

PICTURES TO LABEL

MATCH AND LABEL

DOGS
DOCK
WORM
WORK
HORNS
STORK
WOMAN
HOT DOG
HOT
COLD
GOLF
LOCK
TOSS
STORM

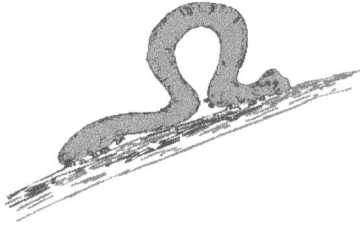

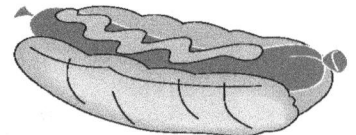

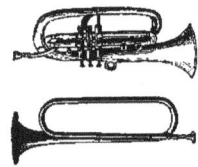

MATCHING WORDS

NOT	WORM
FOR	TOSS
HOT	FOR
LOST	SON
BLOT	NOT
WORM	BLOT
SON	LOST
TOSS	HOT

FINDING THE WORD/READING ALOUD

FOR	OVEN	FOR	TOT
OFF	DOLL	DOLL	ON
HOT	SON	BORN	SON
TOM	TOM	SLOT	WORM
BOSS	TOSS	TOSS	NOT
BORN	TOT	SLOT	BORN
NOT	MORE	SON	MORE
ROT	OF	RUT	OR
OFF	HUT	HOT	NOT
TOT	MOM	BLOT	MOM

FLASH IDENTIFICATION

FAR	FOR	HARM	WORM
LOST	FOR	FAR	ORAL
BOG	COT	CAT	ON
HIT	TOM	HAT	HOT
LIST	LOST	ON	IN
SOCK	DOLL	RAG	DIG
DOG	BOND	DIG	IF
DOG	COST	HOG	DON

SOUNDS IN WORDS

BOG	LIST	DOG	VAST	MOP
COME	BOSS	BAD	FROG	BUT
CAT	DRAM	CROSS	CAB	RUB
SLIT	FOG	SLIM	OR	CURT
FROG	OF	OVEN	GOT	GONE
DOG	WORM	SOCK	LIST	HARM
BOND	WARM	LOST	DOLL	LUCK
DOLL	WON	HOT	SON	BORN

DICTATION

WHAT IS THIS?   CAN YOU MAKE IT BETTER?

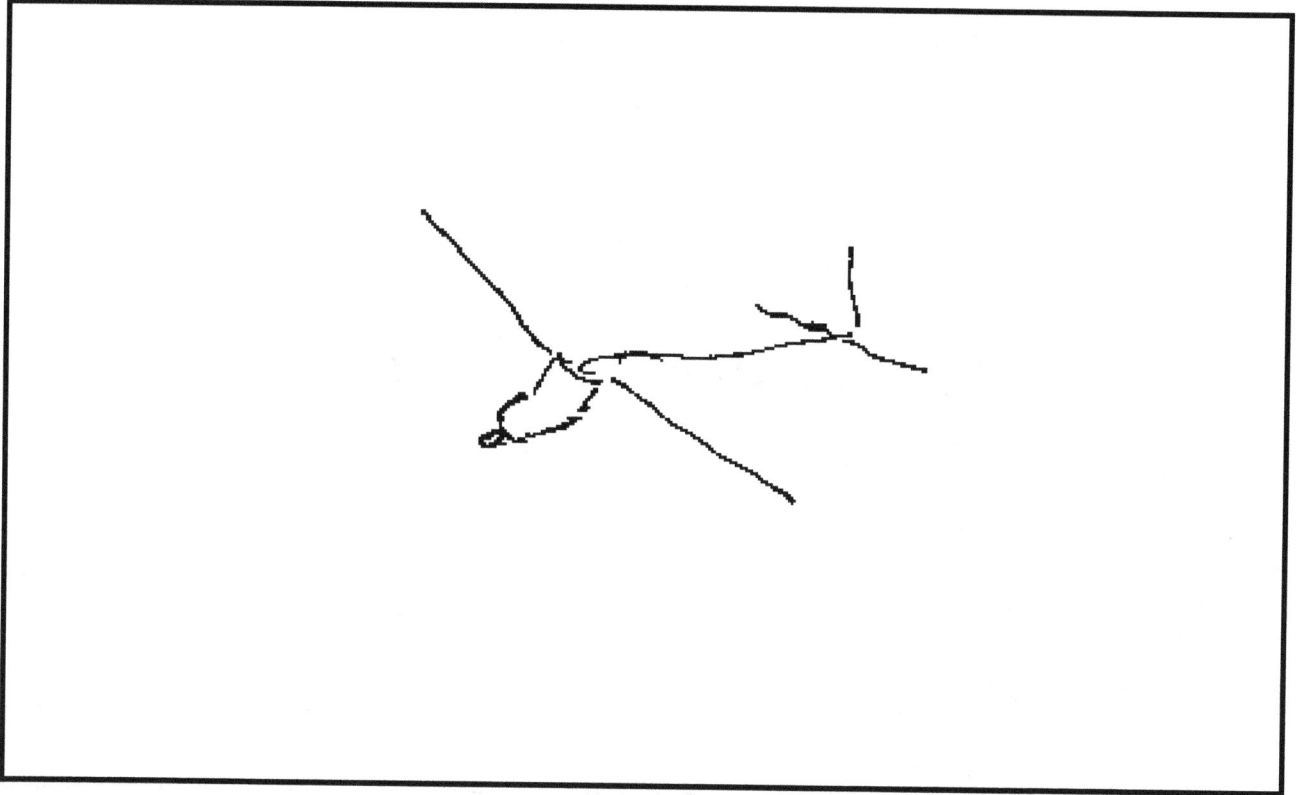

CAN YOU DRAW IT BETTER DOWN HERE?

HOW MANY WORDS CAN YOU MAKE?
O, N, I, R, L, V, A, T, U, B.

PHRASES TO READ ALOUD AND WRITE

A DOG CAN BARK AND WARN A MAN._____

A FROG SAT ON A ROCK._____

A BIRD HAD A WORM._____

NAN LOST HER DOLL._____

A CAR COSTS A LOT._____

DON CANNOT COME._____

A HORSE WILL JOG AND TROT._____

MOM HAS A HOT BUN FOR TOD._____

SAM HAS SOME MORE JAM._____

MOM HAS THE OVEN ON._____

RON WAS BORN ON A FARM._____

TOM CAN HAVE A BUN AND A TART._____

DAN WAS LOST IN A BOG._____

A HORSE HAS GRASS ON A HILL._____

A HORSE HAS GONE TO A FARM._____

COMPLETING SENTENCES

A FR_G S_T ON A R_CK.
RON WAS B_RN ON A FARM.
A CAT WAS W_RM.
MAMA HAS A H_T BUN F_R SAM.
DAD C_LLED A MAN FOR A T_N OF SAND.
SAM L_ST HIS HAT.
A W_RM LIVED _N MUD.

PICTURE PHRASES

HOW MANY SENTENCES CAN YOU MAKE?

DOG	FOR	FROG	AT	BULL	HAVE	IN	BIRD
HAD	A	BARN	WILL	BUN	RUN		SAT
ON	RAT	CAN	NAN	AND	DAN		AFTER
HORSE	WORM	HAS	HILL	HOT	SAW		

Y_____

_____

PICTURES TO LABEL

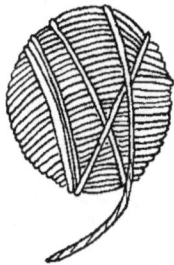

MATCH AND LABEL

CRYING
BOY
WAGGY
KITTY
FUNNY
TOY
WINDY
FLY
BUNNY
CANDY

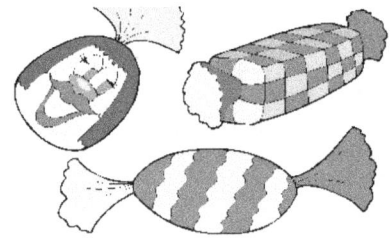

MATCHING WORDS

BY	FURRY
DRY	WORRY
BUNNY	MOMMY
FURRY	DRY
MANY	BUNNY
WORRY	CANDY
MOMMY	MANY
CANDY	BY

FINDING WORDS/READING ALOUD

MISTY	SUNNY	MISTY	CANDY
DANDY	TOY	DRY	TOY
DRY	DRY	DOGGY	INKY
DUSTY	NASTY	BUNNY	BUNNY
CANDY	JIMMY	MUDDY	CANDY
DRY	BY	BY	CANDY
FUNNY	DOGGY	FUNNY	SALLY
WORRY	MISTY	MISTY	DUSTY
JIMMY	DRY	SOGGY	SOGGY
MOMMY	CANDY	DANDY	MOMMY

FLASH IDENTIFICATION

CAN	CANDY	BOG	BOY
WORRY	VARY	WARM	BY
MISTY	DADDY	VARY	JOY
MANY	FUN	INKY	STAR
DRY	BUNNY	MOMMY	WORRY
FRISKY	LADDY	DANDY	INKY
BOY	MISTY	STARRY	DUSTY
DRAG	DRY	TAG	TOY

SOUNDS IN WORDS

DOLLY	BOY	BRAGGY	RONNY	STUBBY
DADDY	CANDY	JOY	KITTY	SOGGY
FULLY	MANY	HANDY	SUNNY	TOY
GLASSY	FUNNY	STARRY	SISSY	TUBBY
RONNY	BUDDY	FURRY	VARY	RUSTY
TIMMY	MUDDY	NASTY	BUNNY	MISTY
BOGGY	DUSTY	GUSTY	GLOSSY	WORRY
DRAG	FRISKY	DRY	MANY	MISTY

DICTATION

WHAT IS THIS?   CAN YOU MAKE IT BETTER?

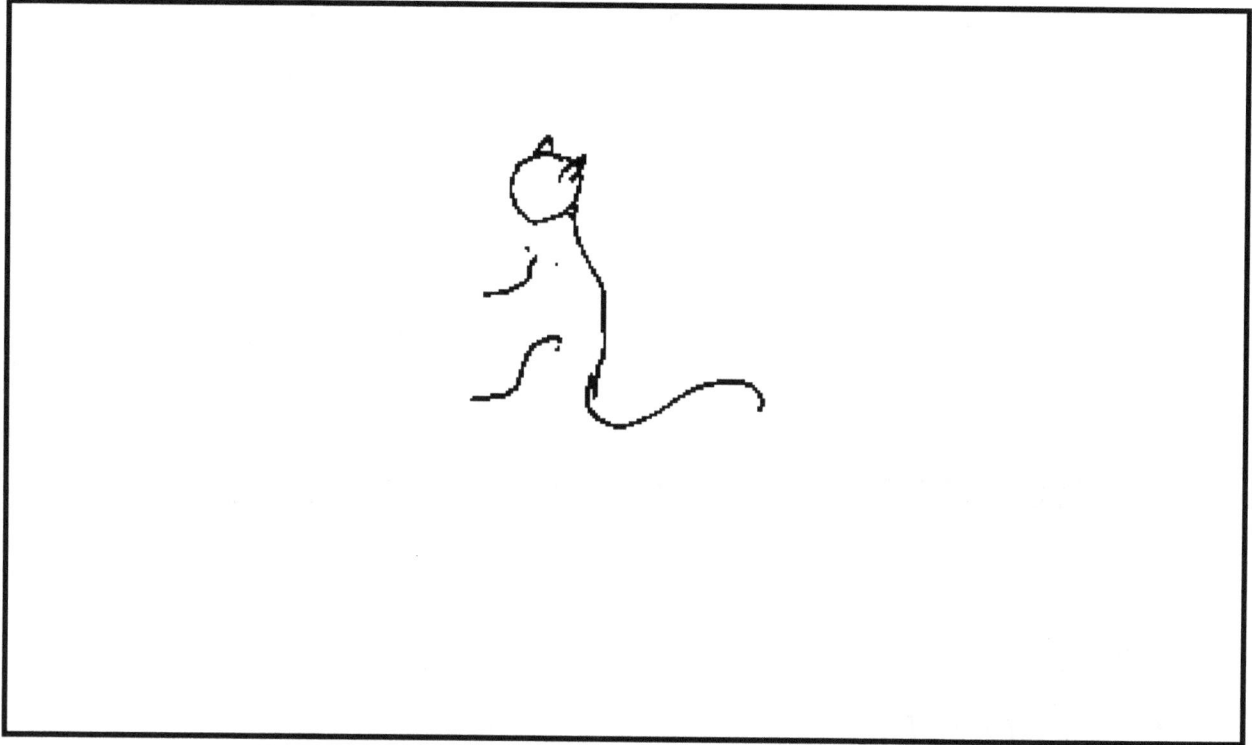

CAN YOU DRAW IT BETTER DOWN HERE?

HOW MANY WORDS CAN YOU MAKE?
Y. N. U. F. R. S. B. G. D, O

PHRASES TO COPY AND READ ALOUD

A BOY HAD DIRTY HANDS._____

A HUT WAS DUSTY._____

A DOGGY IS HUNGRY._____

A FRISKY KITTY IS FUNNY._____

NAN HAD A DOLLY IN A BUGGY._____

RONNY HAD LOTS OF TOYS._____

DADDY IS HANDY._____

A FURRY BUNNY RAN IN GRASS._____

A SANDY LAND WAS DRY AND DUSTY._____

SANTA IS JOLLY._____

MAMA WILL WORRY IF DAN SWIMS._____

MANY DUCKS SWAM IN A RIVER._____

COMPLETING SENTENCES

SAM HAD A FURRY BUN_ _.
A KITTY IS _ _NNY AND _ _RRY.
A FRISKY _OG WILL R_N.
A DO_ _ IS IN A B_GGY.
A _OY IS A LITTLE _AN.
DUST IS DR_ AND D_RTY.

PICTURE PHRASES

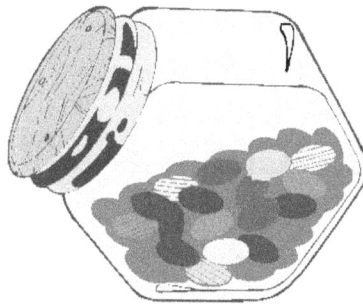

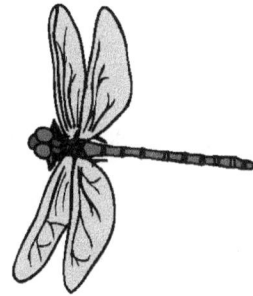

HOW MANY SENTENCES CAN YOU MAKE?

WAS	DOGGY	AND	DIRTY	A	MUDDY	SAW
BUNNY	AT	IN	CAN	FUNNY	KITTY	RAN	1S
SAT	JOLLY	SANTA	FLY IS	NOT	NAN	RUN

P

_____

_____

PICTURES TO LABEL

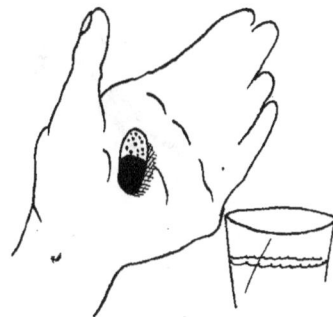

MATCH AND LABEL

CAP
SPILL
CUP
PIGS
DRIP
PRICK
LIPS
RIP
POP
MOP
CLIP
PICK
JUMP

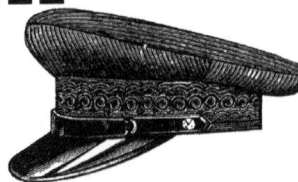

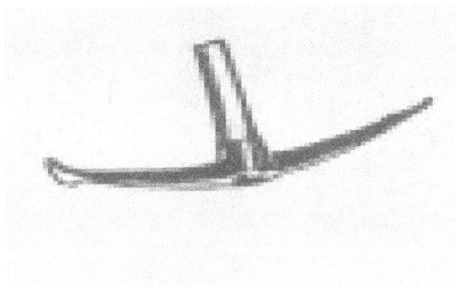

MATCHING WORDS

CAP	PAL
HAPPY	CUP
PAL	SPOT
PULL	PARTY
CUP	HAPPY
PICK	CAP
PARTY	PICK
SPOT	PULL

FINDING WORDS/READING ALOUD

CAP	CAP	PIG	CUP
SPIN	PAW	PASS	PASS
PANTS	SPILL	PANTS	RAT
NAP	PLUCK	PLUCK	SPIN
MAP	LISP	PIG	MAP
PAT	SPOT	PACK	PACK
PULL	PATTY	PATTY	PRICK
PILL	SPUN	SPILL	SPUN
TAP	TAP	PICK	MAP
PULL	PRAM	PULL	LISP

FLASH IDENTIFICATION

PAST	RASP	ROCK	PACK
CAP	PIG	CAB	BACK
SPUD	DICK	SPOT	PICK
PORT	TUG	PART	DOCK
PILL	TILL	DIP	TIP
BIG	PART	RIG	PANT
PAD	LAD	LID	LAP
PASS	CUP	BASS	CUB

SOUNDS IN WORDS

CAP	PIG	CRISP	PACK	PAT
RAP	RUN	SPIT	PAL	LAP
LISP	PIT	SIP	PULL	SPLIT
RUT	PAST	PAN	PIGS	BACK
PROD	RINK	POST	PRIM	SINK
TAP	TAB	PAT	MAD	POT
PASS	CUP	BASS	CUB	PART
SPORT	TUG	PAT	SPOT	PACK

DICTATION

_____

_____

- -

WHAT IS THIS?   CAN YOU MAKE IT BETTER?

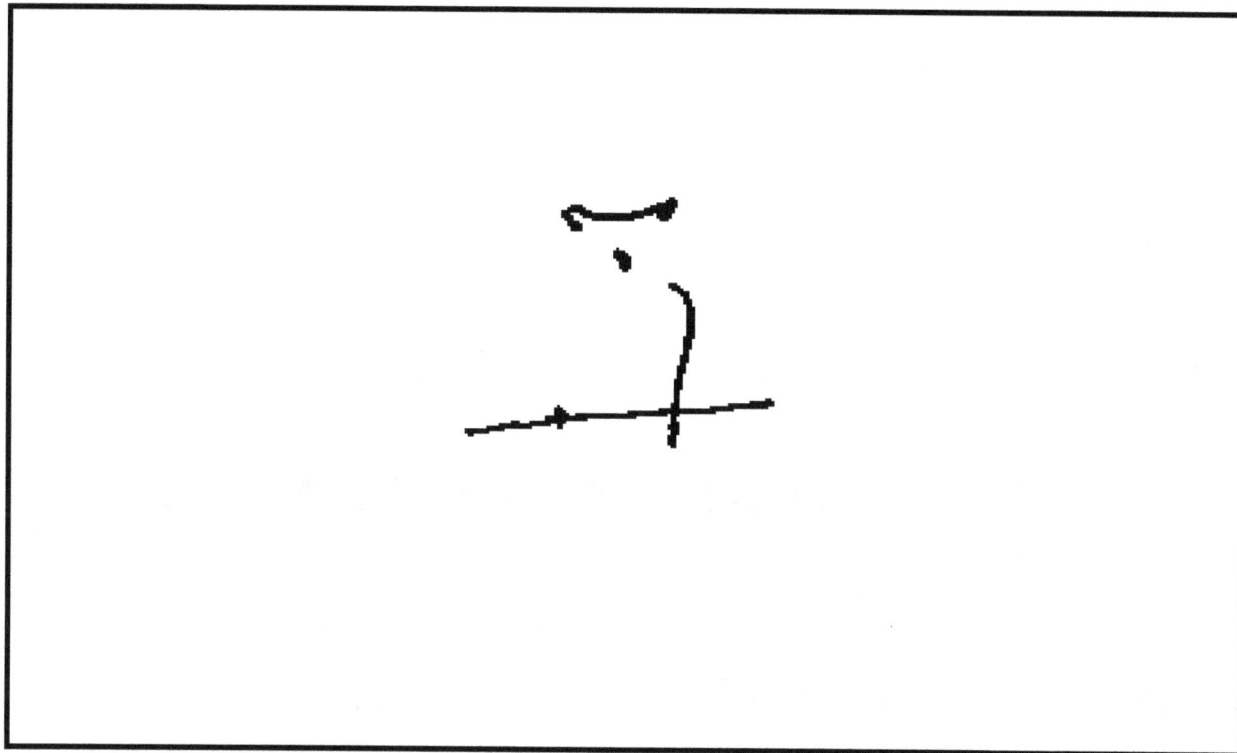

CAN YOU DRAW IT BETTER DOWN HERE?

HOW MANY WORDS CAN YOU MAKE?
P, A, O, R, T, I, N, K, V, Y, U.

PHRASES TO COPY AND READ ALOUD

A BRASS BAND WAS IN A PARK._____

A BUNNY JUMPED IN A POND._____

A MAN HAD BLACK PANTS AND CAP._____

IT IS A PURRY FURRY KITTY._____

SALLY DRANK FROM A CUP._____

PAT LIT A LAMP._____

THE FARM HAD A BIG CORN CROP._____

MAMA PUT A PIN IN A RIP IN SAM'S PANTS_____

_____

TIPPY IS A HAPPY PUPPY._____

DAN AND PAT WILL SWAP CAPS._____

THE POND IS PAST THE BARN._____

DAN HAD HIS PACK ON A WALK._____

COMPLETING SENTENCES

SPORTS ARE _UN.
A F_LL DOG IS A HAP_ _ DOG.
A CA_ HAD A NA_.
A _IG IS H_NGRY FOR COR_.
A DOG H_RT HIS _AW.
NAN P_T A LI_ ON A JAR.
SAM _AD A _IG BALL.

PICTURE PHRASES

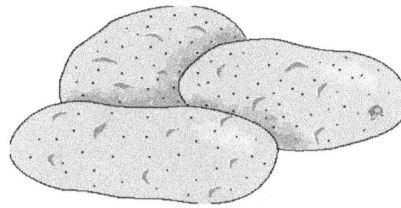

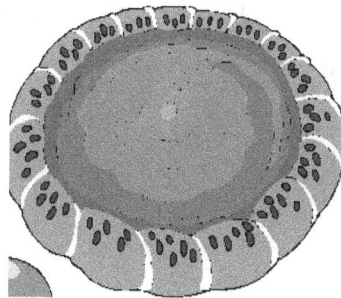

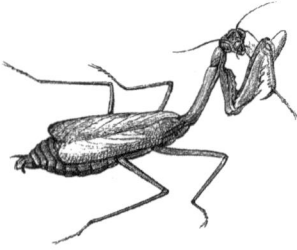

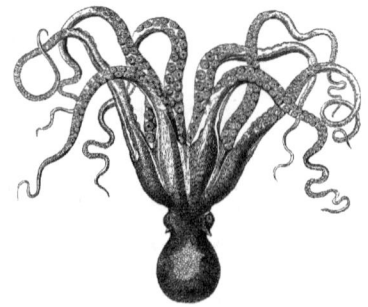

HOW MANY SENTENCES CAN YOU MAKE?

A, DAN   PARTY AND   PAT   IS IN, PIG
HAD   KITTY PURR   IT DIG CAN,
PARK   JUMPED POND   SPOT   PACK

E

PICTURES TO LABEL

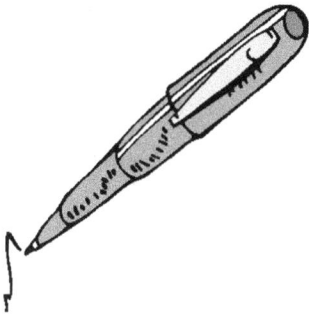

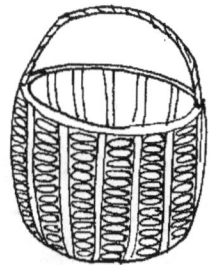

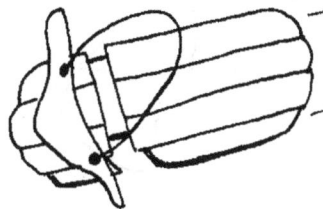

MATCH AND LABEL

BED
HEN
ELK
TURKEY
BUCKET
DONKEY
DRESS
BELL
EGG
KEG
MONKEY
ELF

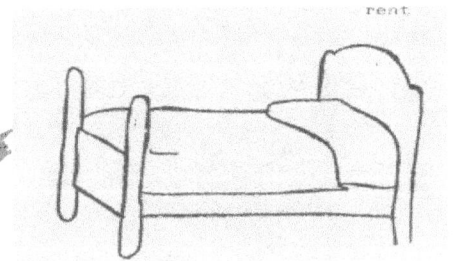

MATCHING WORDS

RED	DECK
DRESS	NEVER
HER	VERY
NEVER	WERE
VERY	HER
EVERY	DRESS
DECK	EVERY
WERE	RED

FIND THE WORD/READING ALOUD

VERSE	EVER	HEN	VERSE
BLESS	SEVEN	SEVEN	RED
END	END	MESS	PECK
HER	WERE	HER	DECK
RED	BESS	DRESS	DRESS
WENT	WERE	BEG	RED
SEND	SENT	EVERY	SEND
DECK	NECK	NED	NECK
LINEN	DEN	DEN	SEVEN
BED	BED	BEG	VERY

FLASH IDENTIFICATION

SEND	SAND	AFTER	AND
BAND	WATER	DAN	DEN
BED	BAD	LID	LED
HER	ELF	FED	WET
LET	DECK	LOT	BECKON
BIG	LINEN	LET	BEG
PEST	BET	BEST	PEG
FELL	WANT	MOSS	FILL
PIG	BEN	PEN	BELL
RENT	LESS	VEST	ELM

SOUNDS IN WORDS

AFTER	HER	ELF	FED	WET
TEN	SENT	SEVEN	BED	SELF
BEST	SERUM	HELP	PEST	PEG
BELL	HEN	JELLY	LEST	STEM
GET	RENT	LESS	VEST	ELM
WENT	FELL	TEST	WET	MEN
WANT	MOSS	FILL	PIG	BEN
LINEN	LET	BEG	PEST	BET
BAD	LID	LED	HER	ELF

DICTATION

_____

_____

_____

WHAT IS THIS?   CAN YOU MAKE IT BETTER?

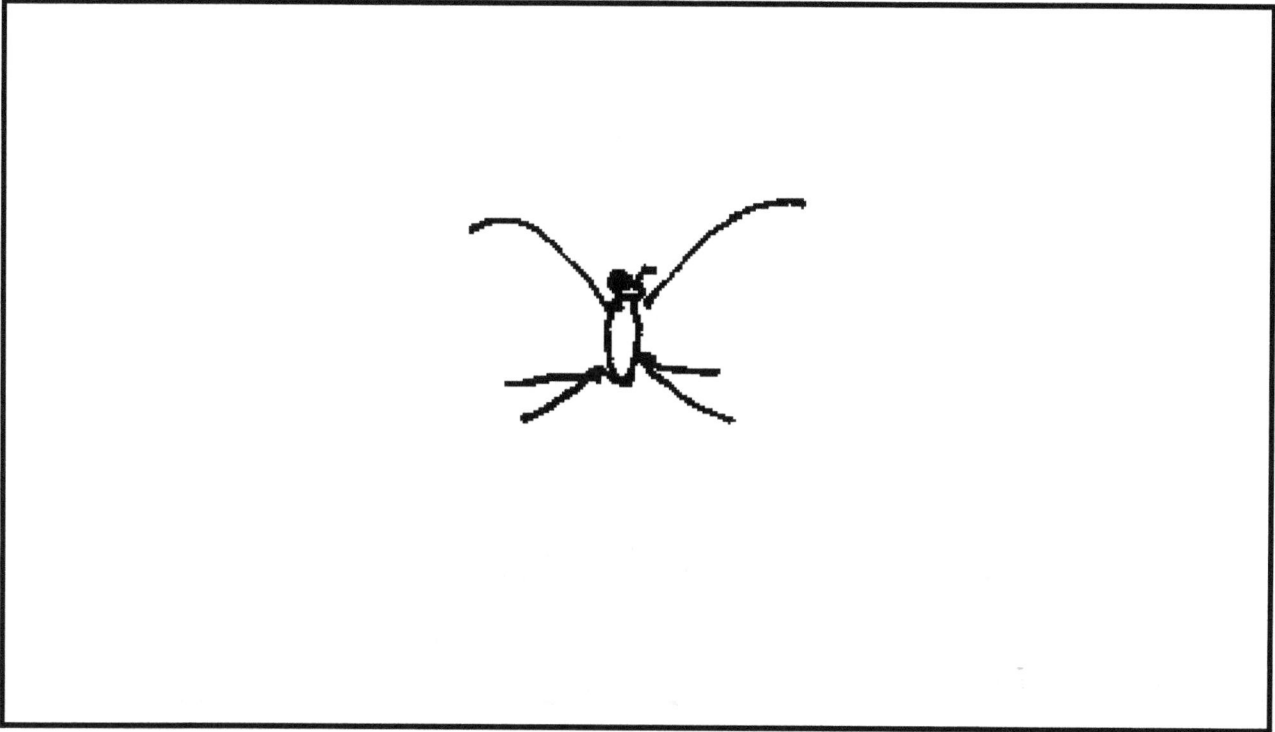

CAN YOU DRAW IT BETTER DOWN HERE?

HOW MANY WORDS CAN YOU MAKE
E, L, N, M, S, T, D, B, O, P.

PHRASES TO COPY AND READ ALOUD

AN ANT IS A PEST._____

A BRASS ROD WILL BEND._____

MEG HAS A GLASS OF WATER._____

A HORSE HAS GRASS FOR DINNER._____

A HORSE HAD A STRAW BED._____

A DOG WILL BEG FOR HIS DINNER._____

SAM HAD A TENT BY A RIVER._____

DAN SLEPT ON A COT._____

NAN HAD HER BEST DRESS._____

HE FED A PET PIG._____

A HEN HAD AN EGG._____

A HEN PUT AN EGG INTO A NEST._____

NAN WANTS EGGS. _____

DAN WILL GET HER SOME. _____

MAMA WILL NEVER GIVE TOM A BAD EGG. _____

COMPLETING SENTENCES

A DOG WILL G__T V__RY HUNGRY.
A P__G IS KEPT IN A P__N.
SAM HURT H__S L__G.
NAN HAS A __ED DRESS.
A W__T BUN IS SOG____.
DAN WAS B__D AND WENT TO B__D.
SAM H__S A BALL AND A B__T.
BILL W__NTS TO VIS__T SALLY.

PICTURE PHRASES

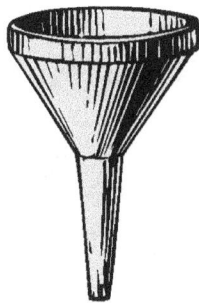

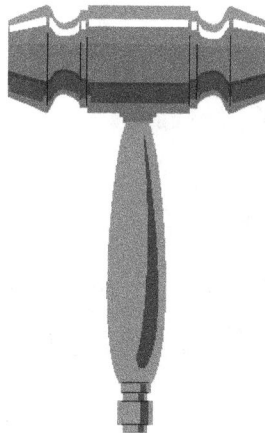

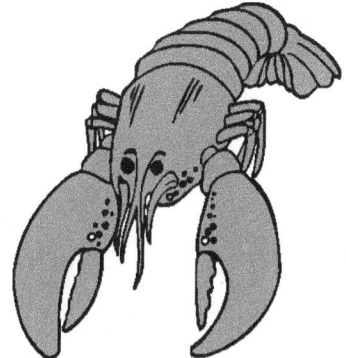

HOW MANY SENTENCES CAN YOU MAKE?

WEST   HAD   IN ELF WAS   AND   NAN SAT
DRESS SENT AFTER PAT A PARTY   HER AN
STUMP NEST   HEN   WENT PECK WOLF RIVER

Z

_____

_____

PICTURES TO LABEL

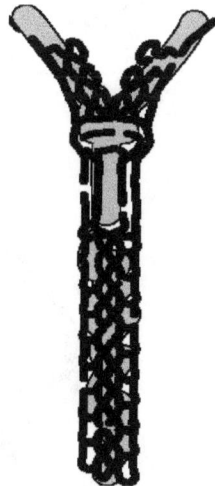

MATCH AND LABEL

WIZARD
FEZ
DIZZY
TOP
PUZZLED
MUZZLE
ZINNIA
GUZZLE
ZEBRA
ZEPPELIN
ZIPPER
FIZZ

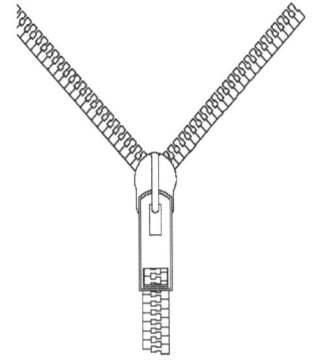

MATCHING WORDS

ADZ	LIZARD
FEZ	FEZ
ZINNIA	WIZARD
LIZARD	DIZZY
ZEBRA	BRAZIL
DIZZY	GUZZLE
DRIZZLE	ZINNIA
BRAZIL	ZEBRA
GUZZLE	ADZ
WIZARD	DRIZZLE

FINDING THE WORD/READING ALOUD

ADZ	ZIP	ADZ	ZEST
LIZARD	GIZZARD	GIZZARD	HAZARD
FRAZZLE	FRIZZ	NUZZLE	FRAZZLE
FIZZ	FIZZ	PLAZA	FRIZZY
ZEST	PUZZLE	WIZARD	WIZARD
BRAZIL	PLAZA	BRAZIL	HAZARD
DIZZY	MUZZLE	DIZZY	MUZZLE
DRIZZLE	ZINNIA	BRAZIL	DRIZZLE
DIZZY	ZEBRA	ADZ	ZEBRA

FLASH IDENTIFICATION

SET	SIZZLE	SIP	ZIP
MAST	STAR	PUZZLE	DIZZY
FRAZZLE	ZINNIA	ZIP	SAND
PLAZA	COST	DECK	MOSS
SEND	LIZARD	ZEST	VEST
TELL	DIZZY	DICK	DECK
LIZARD	LET	ZEST	DRIZZLE
FELL	SEND	WIZARD	PLAZA
PLAZA	BRAZIL	HAZARD	DIZZY
HAZARD	FRAZZLE	FRIZZ	NUZZLE

SOUNDS IN WORDS

ZIP	SIP	ZIP	LIST	SIZZLE
PLANT	PLAZA	COST	PLAZA	AFTER
ZEST	NEST	FIZZ	DICK	FIZZ
FIN	ZIP	LIZARD	SEND	FRAZZLE
PUZZLE	VEST	MIZEN	ZEST	VEST
SIZZLE	GIZZARD	SANTA	NEST	WIZARD
HAZARD	BEND	WIZARD	BRAZIL	BEST
LIZARD	LET	ZEST	DRIZZLE	FELL
ZINNIA	ZIP	SAND	PLAZA	COST

DICTATION

WHAT IS THIS?   CAN YOU MAKE IT BETTER?

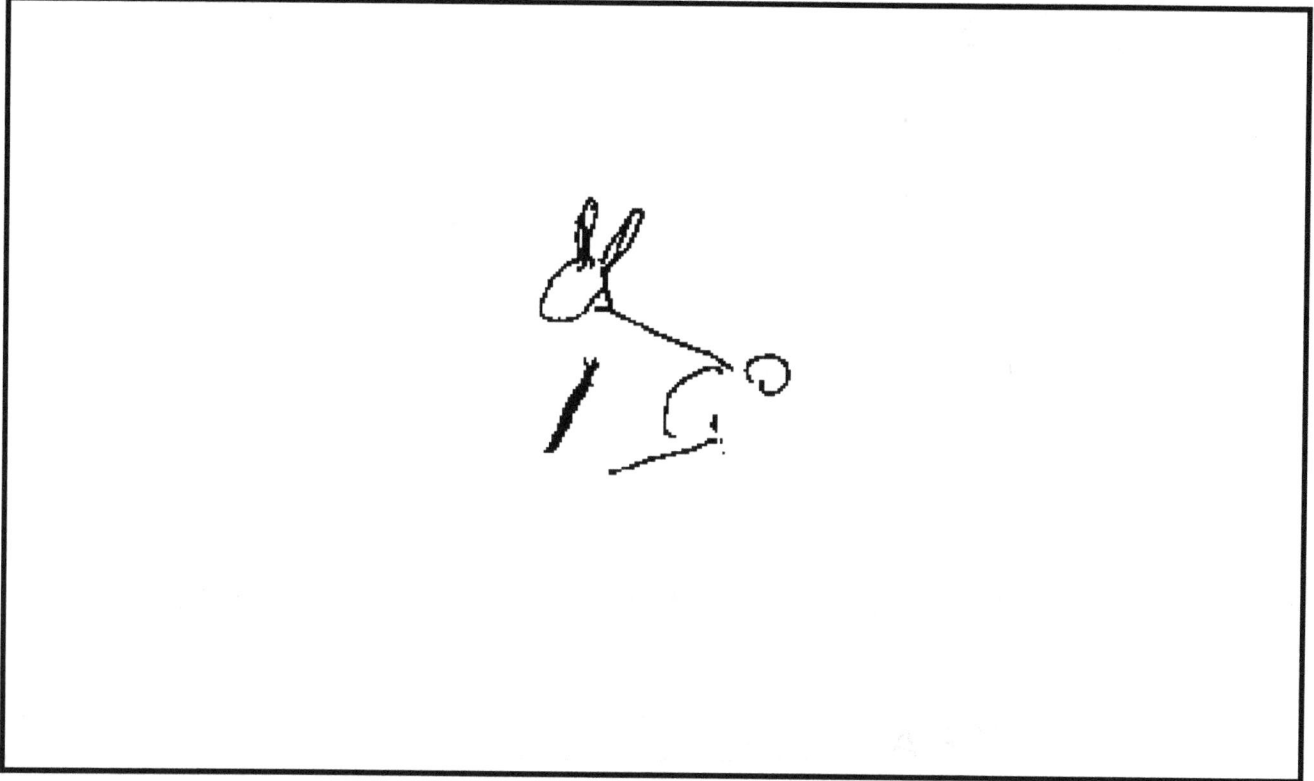

CAN YOU DRAW IT BETTER DOWN HERE?

HOW MANY WORDS CAN YOU MAKE
G, Z, S, L, A, R, N, B, I, E, W, U.

PHRASES TO COPY AND READ ALOUD

SAM CAN GUZZLE A POP._____

TOM'S DOG HAS A MUZZLE._____

A LIZARD SAT IN HOT SAND._____

DAN SAW A ZEBRA IN A HUT._____

SOME WATER WAS IN A ZINC TUB._____

A ZINC SINK DID NOT COST A LOT._____

BART RAN ZIG, ZAG AFTER A LIZARD. _____

TOM HAD SOME ZINC ORE._____

A ZEBRA RUNS ON LAND. _____

NED WAS DIZZY AND FELL OFF A CLIFF._____

JACK AND JILL RAN ZIG ZAG._____

AN ADZ CAN CUT A LOG _____

COMPLETING SENTENCES

SALLY'S BOTTLE OF PO__ HAS A FI_ _.

JAN DI_ A PU_ _LE.

A _IVER CAN BE A HA_ _ARD.

SAM _ILL _UZZLE HIS PO_.

AN AD_ CAN C_T A LOG.

A _EBRA RUNS ON LAN_.

PICTURE PHRASES

HOW MANY SENTENCES CAN YOU MAKE?

CAT   LIZARD   A   RUN   PICK   WARM   NED   IS
BRAZIL   DAN   RUNS   AT   IN BED   UNDER   ROCK
PLAZA   SAT   PIG   ZEBRA   WIZARD WAND   RAT

X

PICTURES TO LABEL

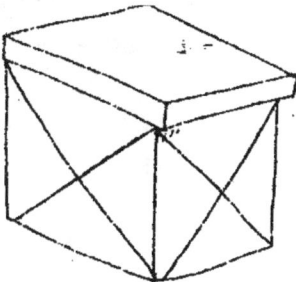

MATCH AND LABEL

OX
SIX
SAW
OXEN
TAXI
AX
FOX
BOX
FIX
WAX

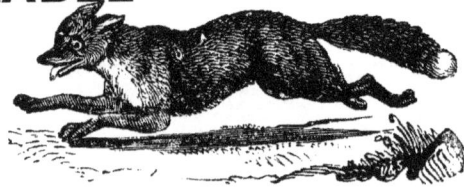

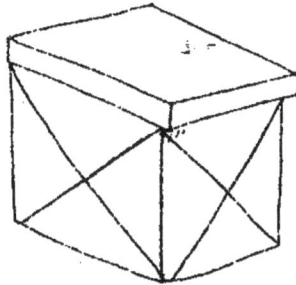

MATCHING WORDS

NEXT	BOX
TAX	WAX
BOX	FOX
WAX	TAX
EXIST	FLAX
FOX	FIX
MIX	NEXT
RELAX	MIX
FLAX	EXIST
FIX	RELAX

FINDING THE WORD/READING ALOUD

EXIST	FLAX	EXIST	BOX
FOXY	BOX	FOXY	NEXT
MIX	TAX	TAX	NEXT
FOX	FLAX	FOX	EXIT
BOX	FLAX	OX	BOX
FIX	RELAX	FIX	OX
FLICK	NEXT	NEXT	RELAX
MIX	EXIT	TAX	EXIT
OX	NEXT	BOX	OX

FLASH IDENTIFICATION

FOX	WAS	OXEN	SIZZLE
FOX	EXIT	BOX	FLAX
MISS	NEXT	LAX	WAX
EXIST	ZEST	TEST	SAX
OXEN	OVEN	SAW	LAX
FIX	NEST	WAS	TEXAS
WAX	BOSS	FOX	WAS
FOXY	BOX	BOY	LAX

SOUNDS IN WORDS

MIX	TEXAS	MISS	NEXT	LAX
WAX	BOSS	FOX	WAS	OXEN
SIZZLE	EXIST	ZEST	TEST	SAX
TEST	BOX	EXIST	BOY	PYREX
OXEN	OVEN	SAW	LAX	MISS
LAX	FLAX	PIXY	LAW	RELAX
WAX	FIX	NEST	WAS	TEXAS
FOXY	BOX	BOY	LAX	WAXY
NEXT	RELAX	MIX	EXIT	TAX

DICTATION

WHAT IS THIS?   CAN YOU MAKE IT BETTER?

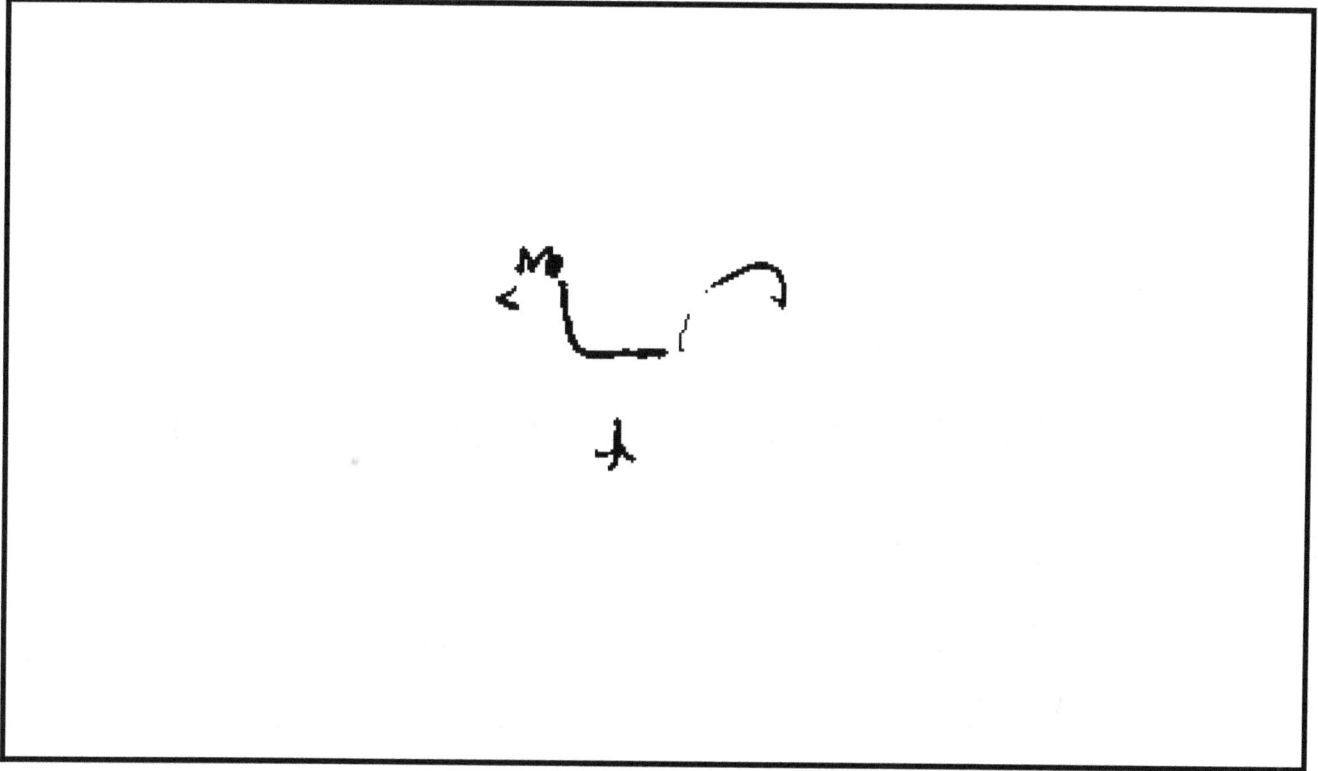

CAN YOU DRAW IT BETTER DOWN HERE?

HOW MANY WORDS CAN YOU MAKE?
I, F. O, X, S, L, A, B, T, E, V, N, W, Z.

PHRASES TO READ ALOUD AND WRITE

JACK CAN FIX A FLAT. _____

MAMA IS VEXED._____

NAN CAN MIX A SALAD._____

DAD CAME IN A TAXI. _____

TOM PUT SOME CANDY IN A BOX._____

BERT CAN RELAX IN HIS BED._____

THE JELLY JAR HAD A WAX TOP. _____

LINEN IS MADE OF FLAX._____

A WIZARD CAN MIX A TOXIN._____

AN ANT CANNOT EXIST IN A BOX._____

TOM FED AN OX SOME BRAN._____

BESS CAN PRESS HER DRESS NEXT._____

GAS HAS A TAX ON IT_____

SALLY HAS A WAX DOLL._____

COMPLETING SENTENCES

A _OX LIVES IN A _EN.
MOM WILL MI_ AN _GG NOG.
BERT CAN RELA_ IN HIS _ED.
A _OX IS FOX_ IN A BOX.
A JELLY _AR HAS A _AX TOP.
TOM _ED AN _X SOME GRASS.

PICTURE PHRASES

HOW MANY SENTENCES CAN YOU MAKE?

BOX SAT ON A UP FIX BOY IN FOX OF WAX
CAN RAN ROCK MILL HILL AFTER LIZARD OX
RELAX DAN OVEN EXIT TEXAS MIX JAM BED TAXI

www.ingramcontent.com/pod-product-compliance
Lightning Source LLC
Chambersburg PA
CBHW081254040426
42452CB00014B/2499